中国思想文化术语多语种对外翻译
标准化建设项目成果

CHINESE THINKING AND CULTURE
MULTILINGUAL TERMINOLOGY DATABASE

中华源·河南故事
CHINESE CIVILIZATION
Stories from Henan

中原民俗

FOLKLORE OF THE CENTRAL PLAINS

河南省人民政府外事办公室　编

河南大学出版社
HENAN UNIVERSITY PRESS
·郑州·

图书在版编目（CIP）数据

中华源·河南故事. 中原民俗 / 河南省人民政府外事办公室编. -- 郑州：河南大学出版社，2022.12
　　ISBN 978-7-5649-5375-1

Ⅰ. ①中… Ⅱ. ①河… Ⅲ. ①地方文化-河南-通俗读物 ②禁忌-风俗习惯-河南-通俗读物 Ⅳ.
① G127.61-49 ② K892.461-49

中国版本图书馆 CIP 数据核字（2022）第 238562 号

中原民俗
ZHONGYUAN MINSU

责任编辑	李　云
责任校对	林方丽
封面设计	翟淼淼
版式设计	高枫叶
出版发行	河南大学出版社
	地址：郑州市郑东新区商务外环中华大厦2401号　　邮编：450046
	电话：0371-86059701（营销部）
	0371-86059750（高等教育与职业教育分公司）
	网址：hupress.henu.edu.cn
排　　版	河南大学出版社设计排版部
印　　刷	河南博雅彩印有限公司
版　　次	2022年12月第1版　　　　　　印　次　2022年12月第1次印刷
开　　本	710 mm×1010 mm　1/16　　　印　张　14.75
字　　数	244千字　　　　　　　　　　　定　价　75.00元

版权所有，侵权必究
本书如有印装质量问题，请与河南大学出版社营销部联系调换。

"中华源·河南故事"系列丛书编委会

顾　　问	黄友义　杨　平　范大祺
主　　任	梁杰一
副 主 任	卞　科　陈　岩　陈志伟　刁玉华　方启雄　韩国河
	惠　康　焦开举　介晓磊　孔留安　李冰冰　李　俊
	刘炯天　李向前　李　镇　梁留科　刘金锋　马萧林
	牛书成　牛卫国　屈凌波　屈鹏飞　史永庆　田　凯
	万正峰　王建修　王清义　王自文　许二平　杨建伟
	杨玮斌　俞海洛　张改平　张俊峰　张明超　张松文
	赵卫东
主　　编	梁杰一
副 主 编	李冰冰
编　　委	陈国良　陈　玮　丁　锐　高　阳　徐恒振　郑延保
	孙立英　郭　远

中华源·河南故事·中原民俗

主　　编	宋争辉
副 主 编	罗家湘　钱建成
中文撰稿	罗家湘　张　敏　霍志刚
英文译者	刘　丹　王　莉　张　瑞
英文审校	[美] Rex Troumbley
绘　　图	严　琰　杨　焱　王梓若　麻梦瑶

The Editorial Committee
Chinese Civilization
Stories from Henan

Consultants	Huang Youyi Yang Ping Fan Daqi
Director	Liang Jieyi
Deputy Directors	Bian Ke Chen Yan Chen Zhiwei Diao Yuhua
	Fang Qixiong Han Guohe Hui Kang Jiao Kaiju
	Jie Xiaolei Kong Liu'an Li Bingbing Li Jun
	Liu Jiongtian Li Xiangqian Li Zhen Liang Liuke
	Liu Jinfeng Ma Xiaolin Niu Shucheng Niu Weiguo
	Qu Lingbo Qu Pengfei Shi Yongqing Tian Kai
	Wan Zhengfeng Wang Jianxiu Wang Qingyi Wang Ziwen
	Xu Erping Yang Jianwei Yang Weibin Yu Hailuo
	Zhang Gaiping Zhang Junfeng Zhang Mingchao
	Zhang Songwen Zhao Weidong
Chief Editor	Liang Jieyi
Deputy Chief Editor	Li Bingbing
Editors	Chen Guoliang Chen Wei Ding Rui Gao Yang
	Xu Hengzhen Zheng Yanbao Sun Liying Guo Yuan

Chinese Civilization
Stories from Henan
Folklore of the Central Plains

Editor-in-Chief	Song Zhenghui
Associate Editors-in-Chief	Luo Jiaxiang Qian Jiancheng
Writers	Luo Jiaxiang Zhang Min Huo Zhigang
Translators	Liu Dan Wang Li Zhang Rui
Translation Proofreader	Rex Troumbley (U. S.)
Illustrators	Yan Yan Yang Yan Wang Ziruo Ma Mengyao

总　序

中国是世界四大文明古国之一，也是世界上唯一的古代文明传统未曾中断的国家。河南省地处中国中东部，是中华文明和中华民族的重要发祥地，在中国五千年的文明史上，河南作为国家政治、经济、文化的中心就长达三千多年。从某种意义上讲，一部河南史就是半部中国史。这里是中华人文始祖黄帝的故乡，是古丝绸之路的东方起点，是少林功夫和陈氏太极的发源地，这里创建了中国历史上最早的都城，镌刻了中国最古老的文字，诞生了中国最初的商业文明。

伴随着新时代的荣光，河南经济社会发展迅速，人民生活水平显著提升，这是河南人民自力更生、艰苦奋斗的历史结果，也是对外开放带来的益处。河南经济社会的发展、人民生活方式的改变都植根于深层次的文化积淀。为了让世界更多地了解河南，让河南更好地走向世界，2018年以来，河南省人民政府外事办公室认真研析了这片古老土地上的历史文化资源和时代风貌，组织各领域权威专家学者，编译了"中华源·河南故事"中外文系列丛书，选取黄河文化、河洛文化、老子、庄子、黄帝、少林功夫、太极拳、中医、汉字、丝绸之路、古都、农业、大运河、文物、陶瓷、青铜器、手工艺、书法、杂技、豫菜、豫剧、脱贫攻坚、空中丝绸之路、航空城、南水北调、中原粮谷、红旗渠、焦裕禄等多个主题，力图以故事的方式向世界展现一个立体、全面、真实的河南。

当今世界，人类文明无论是在物质还是在精神方面都取得了巨大进步，特别是物质的极大丰富，这在古代世界是完全不能想象的。同时，当代人类也面临着许多突出的难题，比如，贫富差距持续扩大，物欲追求奢华无度，个人主义恶性膨胀，社会诚信不断消减，伦理道德每况愈下，人与自然关系日趋紧张，等等。要解决这些难题，不仅需要运用人类今天的智慧和力量，而且需要运用人类历史上积累和储存的智慧和力量。河南历史文化底蕴深厚、包容性强，在今天仍极具现实意义。中原文化蕴含的思想智慧有助于修身养性，推动人类社会进步发展，焦裕禄精神、红旗渠精神所体现的为民爱民、艰苦奋斗的价值取向是构建人类命运共同体的力量源泉。我们期待与读者们一起从河南故事中汲取更多的智慧和力量，共同创造更加美好的未来。

Series Foreword

China is one of the four ancient civilizations in the world, and is also the only country in the world where the ancient civilization has not been interrupted. Located in east-central China, Henan Province is an important cradle for the Chinese nation and Chinese civilization. In the course of the five thousand years of Chinese history, for more than three thousand years it served as the political, economic and cultural center of the country and therefore, as generally accepted, represents half of the history of China. Henan is the native place of Yellow Emperor, the cradle of Chinese culture, the starting point of the ancient Silk Road in the east, and the birthplace of Shaolin Kungfu and Chen-style Taijiquan—typical examples of the world-renowned Chinese martial arts. It was here that the earliest capital city in China was founded, the oldest Chinese characters engraved, and the earliest commerce took shape.

In the new era, Henan has witnessed rapid growth in its economy and remarkable improvement of people's living conditions owing to the national reform and opening-up policy and unremitting endeavors of the people. Modern economic achievements and social development as well as the changes of way of life could be traced back to its traditional values and cultural heritages. To enable people from other countries to understand Henan, and let the Province integrate more efficiently into the world development, the Foreign Affairs Office of the People's Government of Henan Province has organized teams of authoritative experts and scholars in relevant fields to compile this *Chinese Civilization: Stories from Henan* in Chinese and foreign languages since 2018 by crystallizing the excellence of traditions and outstanding features of modern development. The book series include *The Yellow River Culture*, *Heluo Culture*, *Laozi*, *Zhuangzi*, *The Yellow Emperor*, *Shaolin Kungfu*, *Taijiquan*, *Traditional Chinese Medicine*,

Chinese Characters, *The Silk Road*, *Ancient Chinese Capitals*, *Feeding the People—Agriculture*, *The Grand Canal*, *Cultural Heritage*, *Ceramic*, *Bronze*, *Handicraft Art*, *Calligraphy*, *Acrobatics*, *Henan Cuisine*, *Henan Opera*, *Poverty Alleviation*, *Silk Road in the Air*, *Zhengzhou—An Aviation City*, *South-to-North Water Diversion*, *Grain of the Central Plains*, *Man-Made River—Hongqiqu Canal*, *A Model Official—Jiao Yulu*, etc., presenting a panoramic picture of the Province.

In today's world, human civilization has made great progress in both material accumulation and ethical advancement, and the great abundance of materials today, especially, is beyond the imagination of the ancient people. At the same time, however, modern people are also confronted with a lot of problems, such as the widening gap between the rich and the poor, the indulgence in pursuit of luxury and extravagance, the undesirable extension of individualism, the decline of social integrity, and the increasingly tense relationship between man and nature. To solve the problems, we need to draw on the wisdom and powers developed today as well as those accumulated in the past. Henan is endowed with rich historical and cultural heritages characterized by its inclusiveness, and such heritages remain significant today. The intelligence and wisdom in Henan culture are conducive to self-cultivation and to the promotion of social development. The spirit of serving the people and relentless struggle, as embodied in Jiao Yulu and the man-made river—Hongqiqu Canal provides source of strength for building a community with a shared future for mankind. It is our hope that wisdom and strength from Henan stories could lead us to a shared brilliant future.

前　言

　　人类利用语言沟通，形成协作关系，产生认同意识，凝成集体意志，从而有了区别于自然物的社会群体生活。在中国传统概念里，民众在日常生产生活中自然养成的风尚与习俗就是民俗，利用国家力量对民俗进行归纳梳理、雅化提升后，就称为礼仪。以礼治国，又能化民成俗。礼俗之间产生时间有先后，应用阶层有高低，表现风格有雅俗，但相互影响、渗透、转化，礼俗一体，对于社会生活都具有指导规范的作用。

　　中原民俗是指中原地区的民众所创造的风尚与习俗。风尚具有流行文化色彩，传播快，存在的时间短，对人的影响程度浅。习俗是习惯成自然的群体生活方式，形态比较稳定，存在的时间久远，对人的影响程度深。风尚的持续性推动就成习俗，习俗的创造性转化就是风尚。中原民众在其民俗指引下，制造、使用并携带工具，适应、改造并保护自然，创造、规范并认同其社会生活。以当今河南省域为主的中原地区，地处黄河中游的下段和黄河下游的上段，黄土沉积深厚，利于耕作；处于暖温带季风气候区域，春夏时节的东南季风会带来雨水，利于种植。从新石器时代的裴李岗文化、仰韶文化、龙山文化到国家文明时代的二里头文化、安阳殷墟文化、洛阳周文化，中原逐渐成长为人口繁盛、经济发达、文化优越的地方，人们在这里立国建都，进行经济管理、文化建设和政治统治活动，把中原开发成为宜居乐土。中原民俗随着中原人的脚步辐射到周边地区，先在黄河流域漫延，其后随着中原王朝的政治影响力扩展到长江流域甚至更远的地区，成为中国国家文化的坚实基础。秦汉至唐宋，中原地区或为京畿，或为郡县，一直是中国文化的地理中心；

南宋以后，中原不再是中国政治上的地理中心，但仍然是中国人的精神家园，是不可替代的华夏儿女心灵的故乡。

中原民俗的记录和研究有久远的历史。中国文献中早有"民俗"这个词汇，如《管子·正世》："古之欲正世调天下者，必先观国政，料事务，察民俗，本治乱之所生，知得失之所在，然后从事。"察民俗属于政治活动之一。作为被察的对象，民俗记录到多种文献中，如月令类，《大戴礼记·夏小正》《礼记·月令》《四民月令》等，皆属于黄河流域民俗集成文献。地理类，《尚书·禹贡》《山海经》、西晋陆机撰《洛阳记》、后魏杨衒之撰《洛阳伽蓝记》等，包括自然地理和人文地理。郡国志书类，东汉时代，朝廷为了得到地方郡县的归顺和支持，大规模地认定、表彰、征辟、利用各地"节士"，借其家族威重，以绥靖乡里。郡守至郡，首先了解地方风俗人情。就一郡大族节士操行，郡守问、掾史答，一同构成郡国书的基本内容。杂传类，东汉陈留太守袁汤的《陈留耆旧传》开创了"褒善叙旧，以劝风俗"的"耆旧传"体例，紧随其后有各种高士、逸士、高隐、高僧等先贤异人传记出现。民间歌谣类，《诗经·国风》是"行人振木铎徇于路"（《汉书·食货志》）所采，乐府诗是君王"采诗夜诵"（《汉书·郊祀志》）所得的成果。博物类，托名西汉东方朔的《神异传》、西晋张华《博物志》等，影响到后世关于自然、生物、古物等书写，如北宋欧阳修《洛阳牡丹记》、刘蒙《菊谱》，明代项元汴《历代名瓷图谱》等。鬼神怪异类，东汉应劭《风俗通义》有《怪神》《山泽》篇，托名三国曹丕《列异传》，东晋干宝《搜神记》，刘宋王琰《冥祥记》、刘义庆《幽明录》等，皆序鬼物奇怪之事，反映了民间信仰状况。这些著述都属于中原民俗文献。

从未间断传承、长期稳定运行的中原民俗，其功能有三：

一是加强族群认同。人是群居动物，个人必须生活在群体中。自太昊伏羲氏"正姓氏，通媒妁"（罗泌《路史》卷十）以来，中原社会秩序的基点就在家庭。男女两性通过婚姻制度结为夫妇，婚生子女通过冠以姓氏来保持血脉传承。家庭既是一个可以安身的物理空间，又是一个人与土地、庄稼、牲畜共生互成的生活空间，还是一个家人之间情感凝成的精神空间。夫义妇顺、父慈子孝、兄友弟恭，成为维系家庭和谐的重要价值观念。家庭组织具有许多重要的社会功能，如生育功能、生产功能、教育功能、医护功能、祭祀功能等。《周公制礼》作乐，其文化设计的根基在家庭。家为秩序之核，国是家的扩展形式。中原以姓氏为家族符号，根据谢钧祥主编的《中原寻根：源于河南千家姓》（河南人民出版社，1994）统计，起源于河南的姓氏有1834个，在人数居前120个的大姓中，起源于河南的有97个。走向世界的华人家族，仍然以中原为祖居故地，各种姓氏宗亲会返乡拜祖，甚至成为中原旅游的一张名片。在政治层面，新郑每年举办的"三月三，拜轩辕"拜祖大典已上升成为国家大典，把姓氏家族认同引领向华夏民族认同。

二是加强区域认同。自然环境中的江河湖海、高山大漠等隔绝人们来往，生活在不同区域的民众自然有不同风俗。即使是平原旷野，由于人的体力有限，也会形成"十里不同风，百里不同俗"的现象。《庄子·逍遥游》云："适莽苍者，三飡而反，腹犹果然；适百里者，宿舂粮；适千里者，三月聚粮。"农耕社会，出行不便。徒步十里，可视为日常生活圈；百里之内，可视为人情交往圈。远行千里，不是一般人能够负担的。早期人类顺着黄河水系迁移游动，当来到土厚水深的中原时，丰富的生存资源让他们停下了脚步。于是采集、狩猎、养殖、农耕，定居、集会、婚育、丧葬，人们把自己的生活扎根在中原大地，用脚步丈量这里的山川，用汗水浇灌这里的土地，中原大地也外展其深层秘境，展示出无限的包容性，带给人丰厚的回报。中原最大的人造物是城市，在郑州西山、巩义双槐树发现仰韶文化古城，安阳后岗遗址、登封王成岗遗址、淮阳平粮台遗址、辉县孟庄遗址、偃师郝家台遗址等发现河南龙山文化夯土城垣建筑遗址。偃师二里头都城遗址是夏都之一。洛阳、开封、安阳、郑州四大古都，在中国历史上都具有重要影响力，成为整个民族力量的统帅和民族精神的象征。遍布中原的神庙、祠堂、村落、乡镇，就是组成底层民众凝聚力的最基本的单位。

三是加强生命认同。"天地之大德曰生"（《周易·系辞传》），人为万物之灵。人当珍惜自身，关爱同类，还要善待万物。当人类以审美态度看待万物时，物与我"互为主体性"，万物的本性得以彰显；当人类以功利态度看待万物时，万物就呈现出工具性。在具体环境中，人与物都不可避免工具性，体认到工具性对万物造成的遮蔽、扭曲和创伤，有利于修复、修正和共建人与自然的和谐关系。为保证公正客观，中原文化选择了一个物我之外的站位——天道，《周易·谦卦》象辞言其慈悲，"天道下济而光明"，上天有好生之德，降下甘露时雨，万物润泽，滋长繁茂。《道德经》第五章言其冷漠，"天地不仁，以万物为刍狗"，万物各自挣命，不会有谁得到额外的关照。无论慈悲说还是冷漠说，背后的支撑观念都是万物平等。在中原形成的日书、月令、年历类文献都以天人感应、万物同根为其哲学基础，《禹之禁》云："春三月山林不登斧，以成草木之长；夏三月川泽不入网罟，以成鱼鳖之长。"（《逸周书·大聚》）人类不扰动自然秩序，"万物春生、夏长、秋收、冬藏，天地之正，四时之极，不易之道"（《逸周书·周月》）。良好的生态环境必然助成物资的极大丰富，"夫然，则有生而不失其宜，万物不失其性，人不失其事，天不失其时，以成万财。万财既成，放此为人。此谓正德"（《逸周书·大聚》）。万物生成各循其性，各得其所，人顺应事物本性，尊重事物个性，也分享事物的成功。

1846年英国人汤姆斯提出"folklore"这一概念时，民俗所指是原始民族的生活方式，主要是殖民地人民的生活方式。为了开发殖民地市场，人类学学者生活在殖民地中长期观察原始民族生活，记录他们的生活，写成民族志。中国现代民俗学是从西方引进的，清末戊戌变法失败后，人们对帝制彻底失望，于是兴起民俗的研究，要从民众生活中找到政治革命的动力。继承中国古代采风观俗的传统，中国民俗研究主要是民间文艺研究。对于中原民俗的研究，早期主要聚焦于文献整理。茅盾《中国神话ABC》、黄石《神话研究》、杨宽《中国上古史导论》、袁珂《中国古代神话》等对中原神话与传说都做过整理。开展中原民俗调查，1930年代有过，如郑合成等人所编《陈州太昊陵庙会概况》就是实地考察的成果。但大规模成系统的田野调查开始于20世纪80年代张振犁发起的中原神话调查。张振犁所著《中原古典神话流变论考》《中原神话研究》《中原神话通鉴》等成为该领域经典，其团队成员程建军、马卉欣、高有鹏、孟宪明、杨利慧、白庚胜等都成为中原民俗研究的骨干。张振犁率领的中原神话学派形成，推动了河南非物质文化遗产项目申报、中原民俗景观建设等工作的开展。

1972年，联合国教科文组织在巴黎通过了《保护世界文化和自然遗产公约》，其宗旨在于促进各国政府和各国人民之间的交流合作，为合理保护和恢复全人类共同的遗产作出了积极的贡献。中国于1985年11月22日成为《保护世界文化和自然遗产公约》的缔约国，2004年8月加入《保护非物质文化遗产公约》，在世界自然遗产、文化遗产、自然与文化双重遗产、文化景观、非物质文化遗产等项目申报和建设方面取得了突出成绩。2006年至2021年，国务院共公布五批国家级非物质文化遗产代表性项目名录1557项，包括：民间文学类167项，传统音乐类189项，传统舞蹈类144项，传统戏剧类171项，曲艺类145项，传统体育、游艺与杂技类109项，传统美术类139项，传统技艺类287项，传统医药类23项，民俗类183项。河南的国家级非物质文化遗产项目有78项，列入扩展项目的有37项。还有龙门石窟、安阳殷墟、嵩山"天地之中"古建筑群、丝绸之路、中国大运河、太极拳等世界文化遗产项目，都是民俗文化的重要载体。借文化遗产项目建设之东风，当代中原民俗正蓬勃开展。我们的责任是研究传统民俗，调查当下民俗，发掘民间活力，倡导优良风俗，服务于中华民族伟大复兴的事业。

Preface

Human beings, communicating through the agency of languages, enter into collaborative relationships, develop senses of identities and form collective ideologies, thus contributing to the materialization of social community life that is distinct from natural things. In Chinese traditional philosophies, folklore refers to the trends and practices naturally developed in people's daily work and life. Folklore is, in turn, elevated into rites after being sorted, summarized, refined, and improved by exercises of state power. As instruments of cultural governance, folklore influences the people and helps form their moral customs. Although rites and customs develop in a sequential manner, their practitioners involve both the high class and the low class, and their styles present both elegance and vulgarity. However, rites and customs influence, infiltrate, and transform each other. The integration of rites and customs plays a guiding and normative role in social life.

Folklore of the Central Plains embodies the trends and practices developed by the people of the Central Plains. Trends, relishing popular culture, spread quickly and exist for a short time, and exert only a slight influence on people. Practices, the naturally formed habitual ways of group life, however, are morphologically stable and last a long time, thus leaving a deep impact on people. When continuously promoted, trends evolve into practices; while practices, if creatively revised, develop into trends. Guided by folklore, residents in the Central Plains fabricated, carried and applied implements to adapt to, renovate, and protect nature, and created, regulated, and identified with their social life. The Central Plains, with Henan Province as the main part, are situated between the lower section of the middle reaches of the Yellow River and the upper section of the lower reaches of the Yellow River, where there are deep deposits of loess conducive to farming. Situated in a region of warm temperate climate, it receives rain brought by the southeastern monsoon in spring and summer, contributing to good cultivation. Stemming from the Peiligang Culture, the Yangshao Culture and the Longshan Culture in the Neolithic Era to the Erlitou Culture, the Yinxu Culture in Anyang, and the Zhou Culture in Luoyang, the Central Plains matured into a densely populated, economically developed and culturally advanced region. It is here that people founded countries and established capital cities and conducted economic management, cultural development and political rules, revamping the Central Plains into a pleasant and hospitable land. Following in the footsteps of the people of the Central Plains, their folklore spread to the peripheral areas, first to the Yellow River Basin, then, influenced by the political might of the dynasties in the Central Plains, to the Yangtze River Basin and beyond, laying a solid foundation for China's national culture. From the Qin Dynasty and the Han Dynasty to the Tang Dynasty and the Song Dynasty, the Central Plains were the geographical center of Chinese culture as seats of capitals or prefectures and counties. Following the Southern Song Dynasty, though no longer the geographical center of China political administration, the Central Plains continue to be a spiritual home for the Chinese people and provide an irreplaceable psychological harbor for them.

Descriptions and studies of the folklore of the Central Plains bear witness to a long history. The word "folklore" can be traced to early Chinese literature, as indicated by a quote "On Reducing the World to Good Order" in the book *Guanzi*–

> *During the ancient time, those who wish to unify the world and reduce it to good order would make investigations to know state policies, national affairs, and folk customs to master the causes for order and disorder, success and failure, and then they would take suitable actions to improve the situation.*

Surveying folklore is also a part of political activity. Folklore, the subject of this survey, has been recorded in various kinds of literature, spanning the books on monthly climate and phenology, such as *Calendar of the Xia Dynasty in The Book of Rites by Dai De*, *Proceedings of Government in the Different Months in The Book of Rites*, and *Monthly Ordinances for the Four Classes of People*. All these books are the collections of folklore on the Yellow River basin. In the books on geography, folklore can be found in *Tribute of Yu in The Book of*

Documents, The Classic of Mountains and Seas, An Account of Luoyang by Lu Ji in the Western Jin Dynasty, *The Monasteries of Luoyang* by Yang Xuanzhi in the Northern Wei Dynasty, and the like, involving both physical geography and human geography. Folklore is also found in the annals of prefectures and states. In the Eastern Han Dynasty, the court, to win support and obedience from local prefectures and counties, established, honoured, selected, recruited, and used "principled men" from across the country on a large scale, to pacify local forces on the strength of their families. Upon taking office in a prefecture, a prefect first got to know the local customs and people. The prefect's questions, together with his aide's answers, constituted the main contents of the annals of prefectures and states. Folklore also found their way into miscellaneous biographies. Yuan Tang, a prefect of Chenliu Prefecture in the Eastern Han Dynasty, pioneered a writing style of "Biographies of Seniors" themed "Praising the Good and Narrating the Past to Improve Customs", modeled after by biographies of eminent scholars and unusual personages represented by pundits, mavericks, hermits, and monks. When it comes to folklore manifested in folk songs, it is said *Lessons from the States in The Book of Poetry* [1] were collected by poetry collecting officials who held wooden musical instruments on the road to collect poems (seen in *Treatise on Foodstuffs of Book of Han*), while Yuefu ballads were formed by kings who collected poems and recited them at night (seen in *Treatise on Sacrifices of Book of Han*). In the books covering natural history, *Classic of Spirits and Oddities* written in the name of Dongfang Shuo in the Western Han Dynasty and *Record of Natural History* nominally by Zhang Hua in the Western Jin Dynasty, etc exerted an influence on later writings on nature, biology and antiquities, say, books like *Records of Luoyang Peony* by Ouyang Xiu and *Collection of Works on Chrysanthemum* by Liu Meng in the Northern Song Dynasty, and *Chinese Porcelain* by Xiang Yuanbian in the Ming Dynasty. In the books featuring ghosts, immortals and mysteries, we can find books like *Curious Immortals* and *Mountains and Waters* in the book *Comprehensive Meaning of Customs and Habits* by Ying Shao in the Eastern Han Dynasty, *Biographies of Extraordinary*

---

[1] This translation was by James Legge, the original copy is 诗经·国风. Professor Xu Yuanchong's translation for this is Book of Poetry · Book of Songs.

Persons by Cao Pi in name in the Three Kingdoms Period, *Anecdotes about Spirits and Immortals* by Gan Bao in the Eastern Jin Dynasty, *Records of Signs from the Nether World* by Wang Yan and *Records of the Hidden and the Visible Worlds* by Liu Yiqing in the Liu Song Dynasty, etc. all of which, coming under the literature on the folklore of the Central Plains , tell of ghosts and mysterious happenings, mirroring the folk beliefs.

Folklore of the Central Plains, as it has been passed down incessantly and steadily progressed, is imbued with three functions.

First, folklore of the Central Plains helps to strengthen ethnic identity. Humans are social animals, so individuals must live in communities. The basis for the social order in Central Plains, since Fuxi began the work of "distinguishing different clans by correcting their family names and stipulating that marriages must be done through matchmaking" (Luo Mi. Chapter 10 of *Grand History*), has been the family. Men and women become husbands and wives through nuptial institutions, and children born in wedlock are given the surnames that will maintain their lineage. A family is not only a physical space where people can find shelter, but also a living space where people, land, crops, and livestock can coexist, and a spiritual space shaped by family members' affection as well. The husband's dutifulness, the wife's submissiveness, the father's caring, the son's filial responsibility, the elder brother's love for the younger one and the younger one's respect for the elder one, combined, are the important values to maintain family harmony. Families assume multiple social functions, say, reproduction, production, education, healthcare and rituals. When establishing the *Rites of Zhou* and composing Elegant Music, the Duke of Zhou grounded his cultural design on families. The family is the core of order, and the country is the extended form of the family. The symbol of a clan is its surname in the Central Plains . According to the data in the book *Tracing Roots in Central Plains – A Thousand Family Names Originated in Henan* (Henan People's Publishing House, 1994) edited by Xie Junxiang, of the 1,834 surnames with roots in Henan; 97 of the 120 major populous surnames originated in Henan. The Chinese families that have settled down outside China still take Central Plains as their ancestral land. Consequently, the Central Plains have become a calling card of Central Plains tourism industry for Associations of Clans of various surnames to return to their homeplaces to worship their ancestors. Politically, the grand ancestral worship ceremony of "Worshipping the Yellow Emperor on 3rd March", held in Xinzheng every year, has been elevated to a national ceremony, extending the identity of families and surnames to the identity of the Chinese nation.

Second, folklore of the Central Plains helps to strengthen regional identity. People are divided from each other by the rivers, lakes, seas, mountains, and deserts in the nature, which cause people living in different regions to form their own independent customs. Even in the wilderness of plains, the phenomenon that "Places 10 miles apart have different practices and places 100 miles apart have different customs" can also occur. It was said in the article "A Happy Excursion" from the book *Zhuangzi* that

> He who goes to the countryside taking three meals with him comes back with his stomach as full as when he started. But he who travels a hundred li must take ground rice enough for an overnight stay. And he who travels a thousand li must supply himself with provisions for three months. [1]

In an agrarian society, it was not easy to travel, so it can be deemed to be a daily life circle within 3 miles of walking distance, and can be viewed as a people-to-people exchange circle within 30 miles of walking distance. Ordinary people could not afford a 300-mile-long journey. People in early times migrated along the Yellow River system, stopping when they got to the Central Plains , where the soil was thick, the water was deep, and the living resources were abundant. They gathered edible food stuffs, went hunting, raised livestock, farmed, settled down, assembled, married, bore children, and held funerals. They rooted their lives on the land the Central Plains , measuring the mountains and rivers with their footsteps and irrigating the soil with their perspiration. The land of the Central Plains also unfolded to the outside its esoteric landscape, showing limitless inclusiveness and bringing people plentiful rewards. The largest manmade items in the Central Plains were cities, epitomized by the ancient city of Yangshao Culture between Xishan, Zhengzhou City and Shuanghuaishu, Gongyi City, the ruins of city at Hougang, Anyang City, the Wangchenggang Site in Dengfeng City, Pingliangtai Ancient City in Huaiyang District, the Mengzhuang Site in Hui County, the

---

[1] This English version was the translation of Lin Yutang.

Haojiatai Site in Yanshi City, and also by the construction Site of rammed earth wall of Longshan Culture in Henan. The Yanshi Erlitou Relic Site was one of the Xia Dynasty's capitals. Luoyang, Kaifeng, Anyang and Zhengzhou, the four famous ancient capitals, enjoyed great influence throughout the Chinese history, commanding the whole national strength and embodying the national spirit. Temples, ancestral halls, villages, and townships across the Central Plains are the most basic units that build the cohesion linking the underclass.

Third, folklore of the Central Plains helps to foster respect for life. Humans, as written in The Treatise (also translated into *About the Relationship of the Hexagrams in The Book of Changes*), are "The great attribute of heaven and earth is the giving and maintaining life", and are the crown of creation. People should treasure themselves, care for their own kind, and care for all living beings. Humans, when observing things from an aesthetic perspective, are placed in a situation of "mutual subjectivity" with things, thus giving full expression to the nature of things; while when studying things out of their own interests, they see everything as instrumental. In a specific setting, people and things are inevitably instrumental, so awareness of the obscuration, distortion and injuries caused by instrumentalism to all things conduces to repairing, rectifying, and co-building a harmonious relationship between man and the nature. To ensure objectivity and fairness, the Central Plains culture has chosen a stance surpassing humans and things – the way of heaven. The mercy of the Central Plains culture, as described in the paragraph of Tuanzhuan (Structure) in the *Qian Hexagram* (the Modesty) in *The Book of Changes*, reads "It is the way of heaven to send down its beneficial influences below, where they are brilliantly displayed." The heaven, so virtuous as to care for every creature, sends down dew and timely rain, providing moisture to all things and encouraging them to grow luxuriantly. It is, however, reckoned merciless in Chapter 5 in *The Tao Te Ching*, which states that "Heaven and earth do not act from (the impulse of) any wish to be benevolent; they deal with all things as the dogs of grass are dealt with." All things struggle to survive, with none being able to get extra care. Whether it is a merciful viewpoint or a merciless one, the underlying philosophy is that all things are equal. The philosophical foundation for books on daybook calendar, monthly climate and phenology and yearly calendar is the beliefs of interactions between heaven and mankind and all things sharing the same origin. It is stated in *The Injunctions by Yu the Great* that "Axes shall not be applied in the mountain woods for three months in spring for the trees and grass to grow; fishing nets shall not be used for three months in summer for fish and turtles to grow "(seen in the *Superfluous Chapters of the Book of Zhou / the Daju*). Mankind should not disturb the natural order, because "It is the unchangeable law of heaven and earth and the criterion of four seasons for everything to be born in spring, grow in summer, be harvested in autumn and be stored up in winter." (seen in the *Superfluous Chapters of the Book of Zhou / the Zhouyue*) A superb ecosystem will, for certain, contribute to great material abundance, "If so, the land will retain its fertility, everything will retain its function, people will still have their own work to do, and heaven will not mistime seasons, hence, all kinds of wealth will be achieved, to be distributed to people to enjoy. This is what is called pure virtue." (seen in the *Superfluous Chapters of the Book of Zhou / the Daju*) All things are generated in line with their nature and play their proper roles. People comply with the nature of things, respect their individuality, and share their success.

The concept of "folklore", when first proposed by the British writer Thomas in 1846, referred to the way of life of primitive peoples, mainly of colonized peoples. To develop markets in colonies, anthropologists who lived in colonies observed the primitive peoples' life for long and recorded them and worked their records up into ethnographies. Modern Chinese folklore was introduced from the West. Chinese people grew despaired when the monarchy following the One Hundred Days' Reform in the late Qing Dynasty failed. They turned to the study of folklore, in hope of getting a political impetus for a political revolution from people's life. Studies of folklore in China, inheriting the traditional means of collecting and observing folkways in ancient China, are mainly studies of folk literature and art. Early studies of folklore of the Central Plains mainly revolved around collating literature. Collated mythology and legends of the Central Plains can be found in Mao Dun's *The Initial Studies on Chinese Mythology*, Huang Huajie's *Mythology Research*, Yang Kuan's *An Introduction to Ancient Chinese History* and Yuan Ke's *Chinese Mythology and Legends*. The 1930s witnessed surveys of folklore of the Central Plains, for instance, *An Overview of the Temple Fairs at Taihao Mausoleum in Chenzhou* compiled by Zheng Hecheng and others was a result of fieldwork, but massive and systematic field research began with the surveys of mythology of the Central Plains initiated by Zhang Zhenli in the 1980s. Works by Zhang like *A Probe into the Evolution of Mythology of the Central Plains*, *Myths of Central China* and *The General Mythology of the Central Plains* have become the classic in this domain. Members of Zhang's research team like Cheng Jianjun, Ma Huixin, Gao Youpeng, Meng Xianming, Yang Lihui and Bai Gengsheng have become the backbones in studies of folklore of the Central Plains. The formation of the school of mythology of the Central Plains led by Zhang Zhenli has fostered the applications for Henan intangible cultural heritage research projects and the construction of the Central Plains folk landscape.

In 1972, UNESCO adopted the Convention Concerning the *Protection of the World Cultural and Natural Heritage* in Paris aiming to advance exchanges and cooperation between governments and peoples, contributing positively to rationally protecting and restoring the common heritage of mankind. China became a State Party to the Convention for the *Protection of the World Cultural and Natural Heritage* on November 22, 1985, and joined *The Convention for the Safeguarding of Intangible Cultural Heritage* in August, 2004. Since then, China has scored outstanding achievements in applying for and developing the projects of world natural heritage, cultural heritage, mixed natural and cultural heritage, cultural landscape, intangible cultural heritage, etc. Between 2006 to 2021, the State Council released a cumulative total of 1,557 national intangible cultural heritage representative items in five groups, including 167 items of folk literature, 189 items of traditional music, 144 items of traditional dance, 171 items of traditional drama, 145 items of opera, 109 items of traditional sports, amusement and acrobatics, 139 items of traditional arts, 287 items of traditional arts, 23 items of traditional medicine and 183 items of folklore. There are 78 national intangible cultural heritage items in Henan, with another 37 items included in the extended program. There are also world cultural heritage projects like Longmen Grottoes, Anyang Yinxu Culture, "Center of Heaven and Earth" ancient buildings in Mount Songshan, Silk Road, China Grand Canal and Tai Chi (shadow boxing), all of which are important carriers of folk culture. By virtue of cultural heritage projects, contemporary folklore of the Central Plains is flourishing. It is our duty to study traditional folklore, investigate present-day folklore, tap into folk vitality, and advocate fine folkways, to serve the cause of the great rejuvenation of the Chinese nation.

目 录   Contents

第一章　节庆民俗　　　　　　　　　　　　　　001
Chapter 1　Festive Folklore　　　　　　　　　001

第二章　中原庙会　　　　　　　　　　　　　　035
Chapter 2　Temple Fairs in the Central Plains　035

第三章　人生礼仪　　　　　　　　　　　　　　057
　　一、生育仪式　　　　　　　　　　　　　　058
　　二、婚礼习俗　　　　　　　　　　　　　　066
　　三、祝寿礼俗　　　　　　　　　　　　　　078
　　四、丧葬礼仪　　　　　　　　　　　　　　082

Chapter 3　Rites　　　　　　　　　　　　　　057
　　I. Birth Ceremony　　　　　　　　　　　　059
　　II. Wedding Customs　　　　　　　　　　　067
　　III. Birthday Celebration and Customs　　079
　　IV. Funeral Etiquette　　　　　　　　　　083

第四章　建筑民俗　　　　　　　　　　　　　　091
　　一、栋宇住房　　　　　　　　　　　　　　092
　　二、穴居窑洞　　　　　　　　　　　　　　100
　　三、中原古镇　　　　　　　　　　　　　　108
　　四、中原都城　　　　　　　　　　　　　　118

Chapter 4　Architectural Folklore　　　　　091
　　I. Housing　　　　　　　　　　　　　　　095

II. Cave Dwelling   101

III. Ancient Towns in the Central Plains   109

IV. Capital Cities in the Central Plains   119

第五章　民间美术   143

一、方城石猴   144

二、虢州澄泥砚   150

三、濮阳麦秆画   154

四、舞阳农民画   160

五、南阳烙花   166

六、开封风筝   170

七、桐柏皮影   176

八、河南面塑艺术   182

九、苏家作龙凤灯   188

十、修武绞胎瓷   194

十一、安阳苏奇灯笼   198

Chapter 5　Folk Art   143

I. Fangcheng Stone Monkey   145

II. Guozhou Chengni Inkstone   151

III. Puyang Wheat Straw Painting   155

IV. Wuyang Farmers' Paintings   161

V. Nanyang Pyrography   167

VI. Kaifeng Kite   171

VII. Tongbai Shadow Puppetry   177

VIII. Henan Dough Sculpture Art   183

IX. Sujiazuo Dragon and Phoenix Lanterns   189
X. Xiuwu Jiaotai Porcelain   195
XI. Anyang Suqi Lanterns   199

结语   202
Concluding Remarks   203

附录：中国历史年代简表   206
Appendix: A Brief Chronology of Chinese History   206

第一章

节庆民俗

Chapter 1

Festive Folklore

2016年11月30日，中国的二十四节气被列入联合国教科文组织人类非物质文化遗产代表作名录，这是中原智慧为人类作出的贡献。气为万物之本，万物生灭、四季变化是气的运转形态。气要长存久运，就需要有节制有节奏。二十四节气是黄河流域自然气候运转所表现出来的节奏，也是中原人民生产生活经验的概括。二十四节气的每一个节气下都包含三个物候，每一候都有动物、植物、天气等随季节变化的周期性自然现象。在日月星辰规律性重复运动的框架中，纳入黄河流域植物、动物生命活动情态，使中原时间系统饱满起来。

地球绕日自转一周，人在地上看太阳一次升降为一日，月球绕地球

周公测景台

Platform of Shadow Measuring by Master Zhou

On November 30th, 2016, the 24 Chinese solar terms [1] were put on the UNESCO Representative List of the Intangible Cultural Heritage of Humanity, a contribution of the Central Plains people's wisdom to mankind. Qi [2] is the quintessence of everything, and the birth and death of everything as well as the changes of four seasons are the form that qi presents. For qi to last long, it requires restricting and regulating. The 24 solar terms are the rhythm manifested by the natural climate of the Yellow River basin, and a summary drawn by the Central Plains people of their experiences in life and production. Each of the 24 solar terms includes three climates, and every climate involves a cyclical natural phenomenon that changes with seasons shown in animals, plants, and weather. The life activities of plants and animals in the Yellow River basin are incorporated into the framework of the regular and repetitive movements of the sun, the moon, and stars, bringing to pass a fully developed the Central Plains time system.

The 24 solar terms are defined as a day when the earth completes one rotation around its own axis. During the day people on the earth see the sun rise and set. The moon makes one revolution around the earth each month. It is common for humankind to have described time according to the movements of the sun and the moon. Chinese people's understanding of the laws of the movement of stars can be traced back to Emperor Zhuanxu, as shown by the quote in *The Marquis of Lü on Punishments in the Book of Documents* that "Then he [Emperor Zhuanxu] commissioned Zhong and Li make an end of the communications between earth and heaven." [3] A complete calendar was finished according to

---

[1] The 24 solar terms, based on the sun's position in the zodiac, were created by Chinese farmers in ancient China to guide agriculture-related activities. They reflect the changes in climate, natural phenomena, agricultural production, and other aspects of human life, including clothing, food, housing, and transportation.

[2] In traditional Chinese culture, qi(/'tʃiː/ chee) is believed to be the vital life force that flows through the body. Literally meaning "vapor", "air", or "breath", the word qi is often translated into "vital energy", "vital force", "material energy", or simply as "energy". Qi is the central underlying principle in Chinese traditional medicine and in Chinese martial arts.

[3] This quote was translated by James Legge in the *Book of Documents*.

一周为一个月。以日月为授时星,这是人类共同的选择。对于星辰运动规律的认识,可以溯及颛顼大帝"乃命重黎,绝地天通"(《尚书·吕刑》)。到唐尧时期,就依据天象制定出完整的历法了,"乃命羲和:钦若昊天,历象日月星辰,敬授人时"(《尚书·尧典》)。在《大戴礼记·夏小正》中,物候与天象开始结合。西周初期,周公旦在今河南省登封市告成镇建立了周公测景台,以土圭测日影的方式,比较准确地测定了春分、夏至、秋分、冬至的时间。战国时代,一年四季十二月二十四节气七十二物候的配伍完全成熟(《逸周书·时训解》《吕氏春秋·十二纪》《礼记·月令》)。西汉早期《淮南子》的《天文训》和《时则训》有了和现代完全一样名称的二十四节气的完整记载。汉武帝时期将二十四节气纳入《太初历》作为指导农事的历法补充。汉代以来,各种日书、月令、年历成为指导人们生产生活的工具书。春分朝日、七夕观星、中秋赏月,成为官方礼仪的重要组成部分。

登封观星台周公祠
Dengfeng Star Observatory Ancestral Temple of Master Zhou

celestial phenomena during the reign of Emperor Yao, we can find evidence in the quote that Yao "commanded the Xis and Hes, in reverent accordance with (their observation of) the wide heavens to calculate and delineate (the movements and the appearances) of the sun, the moon, the stars, and the zodiacal spaces, and so to deliver respectfully the seasons to be observed by the people [1] ." in *The Canon of Emperor Yao in the Book of Documents*. The combination of climate and celestial phenomena began to appear in the *Calendar of the Xia Dynasty in The Book of Rites by Dai De*. In the Early Western Zhou Dynasty, the Duke of Zhou established an observatory [2] at Gaocheng Town, Dengfeng City, Henan Province, accurately determining the timing of the spring equinox, the summer solstice, the autumnal equinox, and the winter solstice by measuring the shadow of the sun. In the Warring States Period, 4 quarters, 12 months, 24 solar terms and 72 climates were already well-matched (seen in *Superfluous Chapters of the Book of Zhou / Shixunjie*, *The Twelfth Chronicle* [3] in *The Spring and Autumn of Lü Buwei*; *The Book of Rites / Proceedings of Government in the Different Months*). Complete records of the 24 solar terms identical to their modern names can be found in the *Patterns of Heaven* and the *Seasonal Regulations in the Huainanzi* [4] written in the Early Western Han Dynasty. During the reign of Emperor Wu of the Han Dynasty, the 24 solar terms were collected into *Taichu Calendar* as a supplement to guide agricultural businesses. Since the Han Dynasty, various kinds of books on daybook calendar, monthly climate and phenology, and yearly calendar have become references for guiding people's production and life. Worshipping the sun on the spring equinox, appreciating the stars on the 7th day of the 7th month on the lunar calendar [5] and viewing the moon on The Mid-autumn Festival have become the important constituents of the official rituals.

---

[1] This quote is also from James Legge in the *Book of Documents*.

[2] Now, its official name is Gaocheng Astronomical Observatory.

[3] It was also translated as *Records on the Third Month of the Winter Season* by Zhai Jiangyue.

[4] Huainanzi literally means the masters of Huainan.

[5] This festival is also known as Tanabata or star festival.

1. 火历

地球绕太阳公转一周为一年,但是,在地球上的人看不见公转,对于年的把握让人们费尽心思。早期人类通过观察草木的枯荣,判断年岁变化。夏商时代,中原曾有一种火历,以心宿大火星的起落为年时的依据。《左传·昭公元年》记载子产讲的火历故事,从前,高辛氏有两个儿子,大儿子叫阏伯,小儿子叫实沈,兄弟关系不好,经常打架。尧称

商丘阏伯台
Shangqiu Ebotai

1. Antares (Alpha Scorpii) Calendar

One orbit of the earth around the sun takes one year, but people on the earth cannot perceive its revolution, so they had difficulty understanding the basis of a year as a unit of time. In early times, people gauged changes of the year by observing the withering and flourishing of plants. During the Xia Dynasty and the Shang Dynasty, a calendar called the Antares Calendar, established on the basis of the rise and fall of Antares. According to the account told by Zichan [1] in *The First Year of the Duke Zhao of Lu in The Ch'un Ts'ew, with the Tso Chuen* [2], GaoXin Shi had two sons, with the elder named E Bo, and the younger named Shichen. The two brothers could not get along and often fought. After ascending the throne, Emperor Yao sent E Bo to Shangqiu as Controller of Fires to preside over the worshipping ceremony in honor of Antares, while Shi Chen moved to Daxia (also called Ta-Hsia or Batrica) to chair the worshipping ceremony for Betelgeuse. Since then, the rise and fall of Antares Betelgeuse has become the symbol of the year. People in Shangqiu took the 7th day of the first lunar month as the birthday of the God of Fire, and they converge at Ebotai (literally meaning Ebo Terrace) to worship the God of Fire. The Huoshentai (literally meaning Fire of God Terrace) fair starts on the 7th day of the firs lunar month and lasts nearly a month until the 2nd day of the second lunar month. During the fair, people from neighboring provinces swarm to the terrace for worship. Around 4th April, Antares is in the middle of the sky at night, also a time for worshipping. It is another worshipping day for the departure of the God of Fire on the 23rd of the sixth lunar month when people nearby flock to the terrace to burn incense. This fair lasts up to 10 days.

---

[1] Gongsun Qiao, better known by his courtesy name Zichan, was a statesman of the State of Zheng during the Spring and Autumn Period of ancient China.

[2] This is James Legge' English version. Burton Watson's translation is *The Tso Chuan: Selections from China's Oldest Narrative History*.

帝之后，就让阏伯迁居到商丘做火正，主持大火星的祭祀；让实沈迁居到大夏，主持参宿祭祀。东商西参的起落成了年岁的标志。商丘人以正月初七为火神生日，齐集阏伯台祭祀火神。火神台庙会从农历正月初七开始，到二月二方散，会期近一个月。庙会期间，周边数省的群众纷纷涌向火神台拜祭。四月四前后，大火星在夜晚正当中天，也是祭祀时节。六月二十三，又是传说中火神归去的祭日，也举行庙会，周边群众朝台进香，长达10天。

2. 四时八节

西周初年，周公旦通过观察圭表上日光投影的长短，将一年分出四时八节，"凡分、至、启、闭，必书云物"（《左传·僖公五年》）。夏至、冬至即投影达到最短与最长，春分、秋分即投影在最短与最长的中分点。以两分两至为基点再切分，就得到四立："启"是立春和立夏，"闭"是立秋和立冬。"四立"为四季开端，标示着四季轮替、物候转换、气候变化。按照《礼记·月令》《管子·轻重己》、银雀山汉简《迎四时》等所作设计，四立都要举行迎气仪式。迎气用玉，春以圭，夏以璋，秋以琥，冬以璜。举行仪式的地方有堂有坛，以歌舞祭祀迎接四季神灵的到来。自东汉以来，民间重立春，汉代春社的时间在立春后的第五个戊日。春社演社火，谓之"演春"。东郊迎春，谓之"看春"。塑"劝农土牛"（郑杰祥《南阳新出土的东汉张景造土牛碑》，《文物》1963年第11期），腹置麦豆，执柳条鞭打春牛，谓之"打春"。倡优门前致颂扬，谓之"说春"。设大蒜、小蒜、韭菜、芸苔、胡荽五辛春盘，以春饼、生菜、白萝卜、椒柏之酒款待亲戚乡里，谓之"咬春"。颁芒神、土牛画像，曰"送春"。贴青龙于石上，谓之"行春"。

在"四立"迎气之前，春夏秋冬每季之末，都有送气的仪式。迎夏先要毕春，迎春先要送寒。《礼记·月令》季冬："命有司大难，旁磔，出土牛，以送寒气。"季春："命国难，九门磔攘，以毕春气。"

2. 4 Seasons and 8 Solar Terms

In the first year of the Western Zhou Dynasty, the Duke of Zhou, after observing the length of the sunlight projection on the sundial, divided the year into 4 seasons and 8 solar terms. According to *The Fifth Year of the Duke Xi of Lu in The Ch'un Ts'ew, with the Tso Chuan*, "A record must be made at the time of equinoxes, solstices, commencements and closures." The summer solstice occurs when the projection gets the longest, while the winter solstice takes place when the projection becomes the shortest. The spring equinox and the autumnal equinox are in the middle of the longest projection and the shortest projection. Taking the two equinoxes and the two solstices as the base point and dividing them further, we get four "starts". "Commencements" refer to the start of spring and start of summer; "closures" refer to "start of autumn and start of winter". The "four starts" are the beginning of the four seasons, signaling the rotations of seasons and the changes of climate. As prescribed in *Proceedings of Government in the Different Months in The Book of Rites*, *Number VI on the Seriousness of Various Issues in Guanzi*, and *Greeting the Four Seasons* found in Yinqueshan Han Slips, qi greeting ceremonies are held for all the "four starts". Jade stones are used to greet qi, with gui used in spring, zhang in summer, hu in autumn and huang in winter. The ceremonies are held at halls or on altars with singing and dancing to welcome the arrival of the Gods of each season. From the Eastern Han Dynasty onwards, the populace has been valuing the start of spring. The day for the Spring Sacrifice in the Han Dynasty fell on the 5th Wu Day [1] after the start of spring. Shehuo (earth and fire) performed on Chunse (Spring Community Day) is called "performing spring". Spring greeted at the eastern suburbs of the city is called "watching spring". "An earthen ox was sculpted to inspire the farmers" (Zheng Jiexiang. *The Newly Unearthed Stele of Zhang Jing in Nanyang, Cultural Relics*, 1963, NO.11); the ox had peas placed in its belly and was whipped with willow wicker. This event is called "whipping spring". Folk actors and musicians sang praises in front of the buildings; this is called "Telling Spring". People prepared spring dishes of five hot vegetables – garlic, rocambole,

---

[1] Wu Day is a Chinese Taoist term. According to the Chinese sexagenary cycle, it is the 5th of the ten Heavenly Stems.

难即傩，"巧笑之瑳，佩玉之傩"（《诗经·卫风·竹竿》）。方相氏头戴黄金假面，执戈扬盾，四隅刺杀，边舞边唱，索室驱疫（《周礼·夏官》）。

中国古代帝王春分祭日、秋分祭月、夏至祭地、冬至祭天。民间祭祀更重视与春分相近的清明节，与秋分相近的中秋节。二至以冬至为重。冬至日的北半球白昼最短，夜晚最长，称为"日短至"、"日南至"，标示着阴极阳生，一阳复始，太阳往返运动进入新的循环。人们在迎接新生阳气的同时，对于代表开端的始祖也要举行隆重祭祀，合族会食馄饨，"馄饨"与"混沌"谐音，民间吃馄饨，纪念始祖打破混沌、创生家族的功劳。自冬至开始，北方进入数九寒天，人们画八十一瓣梅花，制作九九消寒图。

过年
Celebrating the New Year

leeks, brassica and coriander, and entertained relatives and neighbors with spring cake, lettuce, white radish and jiaobai liquor [1] also known as "biting spring". Presenting the portraits of the God of Agriculture and the earthen ox is labeled as "sending off spring". Posting a green dragon on the stone is named as "operating spring".

The ceremonies for sending off qi at the end of spring, summer, autumn and winter precede the ceremonies for greeting qi for the "four starts". Greeting summer follows sending off spring, and greeting spring follows sending off winter. It is recorded in the *Proceedings of Government in the Different Months in The Book of Rites* that "In winter, he issues orders to the proper officers to institute on a great scale all ceremonies against pestilence, to have animals torn in pieces on all sides, and then to send forth the ox of earth, to escort away the injurious airs of the cold." and that "In spring, orders are given for the ceremonies against pestilence throughout the city; at the nine gates also animals are torn in pieces in deprecation of the danger: to secure the full development of the healthy airs of the spring." The Chinese Character 难(pronounced "nan") is a variant of the character 傩(pronounced "nuo", referring to a worshipping event aimed at exorcising evil spirits and praying for blessing), reflected in the quote – "How shine the white teeth through the artful smiles! How the girdle gems move to the measured steps!" (*The Book of Poetry / Odes of Wei / Chuh Kan*). According to the *Summer Officers in the Rites of Zhou*, Fangxiangshi [2], wearing a gold mask, holding a shield and carrying a spear, plunges the spear in four directions. He sings while brandishing the spear, ferreting about in rooms to drive away evil spirits and pestilence.

Emperors in ancient China sacrificed to the sun on the spring equinox, to the

---

[1] In the term "jiaobai", "jiao" refers to peppercorns; "bai" refers to Chinese arborvitae twigs. jiaobai liquor is medicinal liquor brewed with peppercorns and arborvitae twigs as ingredients.

[2] Fangxiangshi, name of the post of the official in charge of sacrificial rituals and literally meaning a person who sees in four directions, evolved into an evil-exorcising God at rituals in the Chinese people's beliefs. Japan also shares the belief of Fangxiangshi, who is pronounced as Hososhi in Japanese.

3. 过年

年的轮回，代表天时重启，草木再生，这是世上所有生命的大节。甲骨文年从禾从人，会意人负禾，禾养人，禾中有谷魂，年谷丰熟。过年是以人合天，也是以人力协助天时的顺利转换。关于年节起止最长的说法是，"冬至大如年""未出正月就是年"。从冬至开始到正月结束，近三个月的时间，是中国人的年节。民间过年，一般是从腊八到正月十五。谚曰："腊八祭灶，新年来到。"又说："不过十五都是年。"年节期间，中原人家，老少齐聚，祥和喜庆，笑语欢歌，处处都有浓浓的年味儿。"腊"本指用干肉"冬祭"，报赛众神。《礼记·郊特牲》："天子大蜡八。"郑玄注："蜡有八者：先啬（神农），一也；司啬（后稷），二也；农（田官之神），三也；邮表畷（始创田间庐舍、开路、划疆界之人），四也；猫、虎，五也；坊（堤防），六也；水庸（水沟），七也；昆虫，八也。"这些神人物事，对于农业生产都有帮助，故丰收之后都要加以祭祀。中原农家，则以大米、小米、绿豆、豇豆、花生、大枣、萝卜、白菜、粉条、海带、豆腐等原料熬制腊八咸粥，人神同享。

祭灶神
Offering a Sacrifice to the Kitchen God

moon on the autumnal equinox, to the earth on the summer solstice and to the heavens on the winter solstice. Ordinary people set more store by the Qingming Festival (also known as Tomb-sweeping Day or the Pure Brightness Festival) which is close to the autumnal equinox and The Mid-autumn Festival close to the autumnal equinox. The winter solstice matters more than the summer solstice. In the northern hemisphere, the day is the shortest while the night is longest on the winter solstice. This day is also named "day solstice" or "southern solstice", a suggestion that the yin (negative elements) culminated and the yang (positive elements) is conceived. When the yang begins, the back-and-forth movement of the sun enters a new cycle. People, when welcoming the new yang, also hold a grand sacrifice to their ancestors that represent the beginning of human. The whole family gather to eat wonton, which is close in pronunciation to "hundun" (primordial chaos). People eat wonton in memory of their ancestors' exploits in breaking the chaos and creating the family. The beginning of the winter solstice marks a period of brass monkey weather in northern China. People draw 81 petals of Chinese plum blossoms to make a nine by nine cold-relieving diagram.

3. Celebrating the New Year

The rotation of years signifies the restart of heaven and the regeneration of vegetation. It is a grand festival for all the living beings in the world. In the Chinese oracle bone script system, the character nian (year) is composed of the character he (seedling) and the character ren (man), meaning that men carry seedlings, seedlings can raise people, the soul of rice is embedded in seedlings and a bumper harvest will come. The New Year is a time for men to unite with heaven and to help heaven with manpower to achieve a smooth transition. Sayings about the longest New Year festival go that "The winter solstice is as important as the New Year" and "It is still the New Year festival before the end of the first lunar month". It is the Chinese people's New Year festival in approximately 3 months from the beginning of the winter solstice to the end to the first lunar month. The New Year festival lasts from the 8th of the 12th lunar month (the day for the Laba Festival) to the 15th of the first lunar month (the day for the Lantern Festival). A proverb goes that "We make a sacrifice to the kitchen God to usher in the new year." Another saying goes that "It is still the new year festival

腊月二十三是小年，祭灶神，吃麻糖，开始除旧，拆被褥、洗窗帘、扫房子，为过年忙乎。大年三十是除夕，换桃符，贴春联，贴门神，"小儿呼叫走长街，云有痴呆招人买"。（范成大《卖痴呆词》）阖家团圆，说吉利话，吃年夜饭，熬夜守岁，放鞭炮，放爆竹，"爆竹声中一岁除"（王安石《元日》）。正月初一是一年的头一天，春季的头一天，正月的头一天，所以称为三元或三始；因为这一天清晨还是岁之朝（岁旦、岁日、岁朝、献岁、改岁），月之朝（元朔），日之朝（上日、元日、元旦、正旦、正日），所以又称三朝。元旦老礼，鸡鸣即起，穿新衣，放爆竹，拜祭天地家宅堂室神灵，设奠于祠堂祖宗，谓之祝岁。次拜家长，拜亲友，少长以次相拜，谓之拜年（民国五年《郑县志》，1916）。今日习俗则简化为小辈磕头拜年、长辈给压岁钱、上香祭祖、吃饺子等。初一到十五，都是团聚宴会的日子，人神禽兽共享丰收成果，共享生命盛宴。一鸡二犬三猪四羊五牛六马七人八蚕九龙十虎十一猫

孔明灯
Kongming Lantern

until the Lantern Festival." During the New Year festival, people in the Central Plains, old and young, gather in an atmosphere of peace and jubilation, singing and laughing, with strong festive vibes felt everywhere. The Chinese character 腊(pronounced as xi or la) refers to an event in which dried meat is used for the winter solstice worshipping in return for all the Gods. A sentence in *The Great Suburban Sacrifice in the Book of Rites* reads "The great ji [1] sacrifice of the son of Heaven consisted of eight sacrifices." According to Zheng Xuan's annotations, "The La sacrifice event includes eight sacrifices. The first is for Xianse (also called Shennong / The Divine Farmer); the second for Sise (also called Houji / Lord of Millet Grains)"; the third for Nong (God of Farmers); the fourth for Youbiaochuo (referring to those who built houses, roads and demarcated borderlines); the fifth for cats and tigers; the sixth for embankment; the seventh for water channels; and the eighth for insects." All the gods, people and things mentioned are conducive to agrarian production, so they are all worshipped after harvest. Farmers in the Central Plains cook Laba salty porridge with rice, millet, mung beans, cowpeas, peanuts, jujubes, radishes, cabbage, rice noodles, kelp, tofu (beancurd) and other raw materials, to be shared by both mortals and gods. The 23rd day of the 12th lunar month is the Minor New Year' Day when people sacrifice to the Kitchen God, eat sesame candy, and begin to ring out the old by changing the bedding, cleaning the curtains, and sweeping out rooms, having their hands full with the preparation for the new year. The new year's eve falls on the 30th of the 12th lunar month when people replace the peach wood charms, post the Spring Festival couplets and portraits of Door Gods, as is shown in the line – "The kids are walking and crying in the main street, inquiring if anyone can buy their imbecility" (in Fan Chengda's poem – *Clearing Away Imbecility*). Family members get together, say auspicious words, have New Year's Eve dinner, stay up for the arrival of the New Year, and set off firecrackers. Wang Anshi depicted this in his poem *New Year's Day* [2] : "The old year concludes amid the boom of firecrackers." Lunar New Year's Day is the first day of a year, the first day of spring and the first

---

[1] "ji" here is another spelling of the word 腊(pronounced as xi or la in modern Chinese).

[2] China's lunar new year.

十二鼠十三十四抱鸡母（一说十三皮蜂十四虼蚤），所有的生灵都得到专门回报。正月十五元宵节，吃元宵、放烟花、猜灯谜、赏花灯、赏月、看戏、闹社火，人神同乐。

4. 清明节

清明节时令在仲春与暮春之交，又称踏青节、祭祖节等。清明时节，气温升高，雨水增多，春和景明，万物洁齐，正是外出游赏好时节。离家外出，就有熄灭旧火、改生新火的需要。清明节改火、寒食的习俗来源于寒食节。传说寒食节是为纪念春秋时代晋国忠臣介子推而设立的节日，其实这是世界性的习俗，有更古老的来源。《论语·阳货》"钻燧

清明节踏青郊游
Going on a Spring Outing on the Qingming Festival

day of the first lunar month, so it is also called Three Firsts or Three Beginnings. Furthermore, because the morning of Lunar New Year's Day is the break of year (named Suidan, Suiri, Suizhao, Xiansui and Gaisui in different periods of history), the break of month and the break of day (named yuanshuo), it is also called Three Breaks (named Shangri, Yuanri, Yuandan, Zhengdan, Zhengri in different periods of history). It was the old practice for people on the Lunar New Year's Day to get up at cockcrow, put on new clothes, light off firecrackers, make sacrificial offerings to heaven, earth and gods of houses and halls, worship ancestors at the ancestral hall, which was called New Year Greeting. Then people pay tribute to their parents and to their relatives and friends; the younger ones pay tribute to the older and the older return their respect, as is called New Year Tribute (*Chronicles of Zheng County*, 1916). Now the practice has been simplified; the juniors genuflect and pay tribute to the seniors, who return with lucky money; people burn incense to worship ancestors and have dumplings. From the first day to the 15th day of the lunar New Year, every day is for reunion and banquets. People, gods, fowls, and animals share the fruits of harvest and enjoy the feast of life. All the living creatures (14 creatures in total, they are chickens, dogs, pigs, sheep, oxen, horses, men, silkworms, dragons, tigers, cats, rats and broody hens (or wood wasps and fleas in place of broody hens in some editions)) get special returns. On the Lantern Festival, people eat yuanxiao (the old spelling is Yuanhsiao), set off fireworks, guess lantern riddles, watch decorative lanterns, view the moon, watch dramas, and observe shehuo. Mortals and gods rejoice together.

4. The Qingming Festival

The Qingming Festival, which falls at the junction of mid spring and late spring, is also styled the Hiking Festival and the Ancestral Festival. The festival is a good time for outings, for in this period, the temperature rises, the rainfall increases, the weather is mild, and the entire scene brightens. When people go out of their homes, it is necessary to put out the old fire and make a new fire. Renewing the fire and eating cold food originated from the Cold Food Festival. Legend has it that the Cold Food Festival was established commemorative of Jie Zitui, a loyal minister who served the State of Jin during the Spring and Autumn Period, but in reality it is a worldwide custom with a much older origin.

改火",刘宝楠正义引徐颋《改火解》云:"改火之典,昉於上古,行於三代,迄於汉,废於魏晋以后,复於隋而仍废。"(刘宝楠《论语正义》,上海书店1986年影印诸子集成本,第381页)火能驱寒,能加热食物,对人类的生存起到重要支撑作用。但火也能烧伤人体,烧毁财物,带给人类巨大伤害。通过改火,既去旧火之毒,又传取火之术,对人类的发展是有好处的。旧火已灭,新火未生,其间禁烟火、吃冷食,人们趁机上坟祭扫,在野外从事秋千、蹴鞠、牵勾、斗鸡等活动。

清明节祓禊宴饮的习俗源于上巳节。三月上旬的第一个巳日,谓之"上巳"。上巳节,俗称三月三,人们结伴去水边祓禊,曲水流觞,借助春水的力量祓除不祥。《晋书·列传第二十一》记载挚虞与束皙关于上巳节"三日曲水"风俗起源的争议。周公城洛邑时泛酒流水说,秦昭王置酒河曲说,后汉避产鬼说等,强调了祓禊去疾病、避产鬼、聚大众、宴宾客等功用,显示了祓禊的扩散变异过程和它的巨大影响力。从东汉杜笃《祓禊赋》《禊祝》,蔡邕《祓禊文》,西晋成公绥《洛禊赋》,

清明节扫墓
Tomb-sweeping on the Qingming Festival

An expression – "procuring fire by friction" can be found in the *Yang Huo* in *The Analects*. Liu Baonan (also spelt as Pao-nan Liu), in his book – Correct Meaning of The Analects, cited Xu Ting's *An Interpretation of Renewing Fire* as saying that "The practice of renewing fire stemmed from time immemorial, prevailed in the Xia Dynasty, the Shang Dynasty and the Zhou Dynasty until the Han Dynasty, phased out after the Wei, Jin, and Southern and Northern Dynasties, reemerged in the Sui Dynasty and is now disused again." (Liu Baonan, *Photocopied Collections of Philosophical Schools of Thought*, Shanghai Bookstore, 1986, p. 381) Fire can repel cold, heat food, thus playing an important role in securing human beings' survival. It, however, can also burn human bodies, burn up properties, bringing great harm to mankind. Renewing fire cannot only rid the old fire of blight but can pass the art of making fire down as well, which benefits the development of humans. The old fire has been put out, while the new fire has not been made, during which time, fire is prohibited, and only cold food is available. People take this opportunity to pay tribute to their ancestral tombs and do some sweeping, and participate in such events afield as swinging, *cuju* (an ancient Chinese football game) playing, tug of war and cockfighting.

The customs of Fuxi (Purification) [1] and feasting on the Qingming Festival originated from the Shangsi Festival (also known as March 3 Festival, Double Third Festival). The first Si [2] Day of early March is called "Upper Si". On the Shangsi Festival, commonly known as March 3rd, people go to the waterside for the Fuxi ritual. Wine vessels are set afloat and drift down the stream, and the inauspiciousness is extirpated with the aid of the spring water. According to the *Biography 21* in the *Collective Biographies* in the *Book of Jin*, there was a dispute between Zhi Yu and Shu Xi over the origin of the custom of "circular waterway drinking game on the third day of the third month". There are different versions of the origin, say, the Duke of Zhou set goblets afloat the stream when finishing the construction of the Luoyi City, the King Zhaoxiang of Qin held a feast at

---

[1] This is a ritual during the process of which people exorcise the evil by cleaning their bodies in the water.

[2] Si Day is a Chinese Taoist term. According to the Chinese sexagenary cycle, it is the 6th of the ten Heavenly Stems.

褚爽《禊赋》，夏侯湛《禊赋》，张协《禊赋》等直接以被禊为标题的作品看，上巳节被禊是东汉以来盛行的风俗。

〔唐〕杜牧《清明》诗写道："清明时节雨纷纷，路上行人欲断魂。"清明节从唐代以来就是重要节日，扫墓祭祖与踏青郊游是清明节的两大礼俗主题。这样的主题在七月十五日中元节、十月一日寒衣节不断重复，显示了中原人民对孝道亲情的重视。亲近自然，不忘先烈，这是中华民族的优良传统，有利于提升民族凝聚力和认同感。2006年，清明节列入第一批国家级非物质文化遗产名录。2008年，清明节正式成为国家法定节假日。

5. 端午节

端午节又名端阳节、重五节、天中节、龙舟节、女儿节、诗人节等，别称多达20多个。中原民俗对于农历数字有一种神秘观念，认为单月与单日数字相同，这一天就具有特别意义。一月一日春节驱山臊恶鬼，三月三日上巳节度产厄，五月五日端午节除害虫，七月七日七夕节解别

端午节赛龙舟
Dragon Boat Race on the Dragon Boat Festival

the bend of a river, and people expelled childbirth demons in the Eastern Han Dynasty. All the versions lay emphasis on removing diseases, expelling childbirth demons, converging people and entertain guests, indicative of the process of proliferation and evolution of Fuxi and its huge influence. From the books titled Fuxi like the *Ode to Fuxi* and the *Celebrating Fuxi* by Du Du and the *An Account of Fuxi* by Cai Yong in the Eastern Dynasty, and the *Ode to Fuxi* in Luoyang by Cheng Gongsui, the *Ode to Fuxi* by Chu Shuang, the *Ode to Fuxi* by Xiahou Zhan and the *Ode to FuXi* by Zhang Xie in the Western Jin Dynasty, etc. we can know the custom of FuXi on Shangsi Festival has been the most prevailing since the Eastern Han Dynasty.

A line in the poem – *Qingming* by Du Mu, a poet in the Tang Dynasty, tells that "It is Qingming, early April, a season of mizzle and gloom, Away from home, a wayfarer, faring into gloom and doom [1] ." The Qingming Festival has been an important festival since the Tang Dynasty, with tomb-sweeping and ancestral worship and hiking as the two major customary themes. Themes of this kind recur on the Ghost Festival (the 15th day of the 7th lunar month) and the Winter Clothing Festival (also known as Winter Clothes Day that falls on the 1st day of the 10th lunar month), a sign of the importance people in the Central Plains attach to filial piety and affection between family members and between relatives. It is the fine tradition of Chinese nation to get close to the nature and bear in mind our ancestors, and this tradition helps to enhance national cohesion and national identity. In 2006, the Qingming Festival was put on The First National List of Intangible Cultural Heritage of China. In 2008, the Qingming Festival was designated as a national holiday by the Chinese government.

5. The Dragon Boat Festival

The Dragon Boat Festival is also known as Duanyang Festival (Bright Sun Festival), Chongwu Festival (Double Five Festival), Tianzhong Festival (Mid-sky Festival), Duanwu Festival (Fifth Month Festival), Daughters' Festival and Poets' Festival, etc. and by more than 20 other names. There is a mysterious belief about the lunar numbers in folklore of the Central Plains, which holds that if

---

[1] This is from the translation by Andrew W.F. Wong (Huang Hongfa).

离之苦,九月九日重阳节避水灾,"这些同样数字重复的节日都是奇数,而奇一般有特殊、出人意料、令人惊异之义,更有不和谐、不适应、不顺遂之义"。刘晓峰发现,以端午节为基点,"前半年的一月一日登高、三月三日临水,和后半年七月七日临水、九月九日登高,这中间存在着整齐的对称关系。而排在中间的五月五日则可登高可临水"。汉代将五月五日看作恶月恶日,有毒虫之害,瘟疫之灾,五月五日出生的婴儿也不能抚养成人,否则男害父,女害母。为禳灾逐疫,要门挂蒲艾,煮大蒜,吃粽子,饮雄黄酒,系五色丝线,上山采百草,下河龙舟竞渡。端午节又是传递婚姻信息的节日,有情男女相互致送果品衣物以表情意,谓之追节。托媒说亲要上一篮粽子,拎一提鸭蛋,加上几斤肉和挂面等八样礼;准女婿上门,一般送上夏日用物,竹凉席一床、扇子若干、阉割过的大公鸡一只、粽子一匹十个等。除端午外,六月六天贶节、八月十五中秋节、九九重阳节、十一月冬至节等也是姻亲交往的追节。2006年,端午民俗列入我国第一批国家级非物质文化遗产名录。自2008年开始,

端午节吃粽子
Eating Zongzi on the Dragon Boat Festival

the number of the odd-numbered day is the same as that of the odd-numbered month, then the day is of special significance. On the 1st day of the 1st lunar month (the Spring Festival), the mountain demons are exorcised; on the 3rd day of the 3rd lunar month (the Shangsi Festival), the childbirth demons are repelled; on the 5th day of the 5th lunar month (the Dragon Boat Festival), pests are done away with; on the 7th day of the 7th month (the Qixi Festival, the Chinese Saint Valentine's Day), the pain of separation between lovers is relieved; on the 9th day of the 9th lunar month (the Double Ninth Festival), people climb to a height to avoid floods. All these repeated numbers of the festivals are odd numbers ("jishu" in Chinese). The Chinese character "ji" (odd) refers not only to the connotations of "special", "unexpected" and "surprising", but more of "disharmonious", "inadaptable" and "unsmooth". As indicated in Liu Xiaofeng's findings, taking the Dragon Boat Festival as the base point, we will find that "In the first half of a year, people ascend to a height on the 1st day of the first lunar month and approach to the waterside on the 3rd of the 3rd lunar month; in the second half of a year, people approach to the waterside on the 7th day of the 7th month and ascend to a height on the 9th day of the 9th lunar month. There is a complete symmetry between the two halves; while on the 5th day of the 5th lunar month that is in the middle, people can climb a mountain and visit a waterfront as well." The 5th day of the 5th lunar month in the Han Dynasty was considered the evil day of the vicious month plagued by noxious insects and epidemics. Babies born on that day could not be raised into adulthood, otherwise, sons would harm their fathers, and daughters harm their mothers. To stave off disasters and pestilences, people hung wormwood on the door, boil garlic, eat *zongzi*, drink realgar wine, wear five-colored ribbons, gather multifarious medicinal herbs in the mountain and take part in the dragon boat race in the river. For the Dragon Boat Festival is also a festival for communicating messages of marriage, boys and girls taking a fancy to each other exchange fruits and clothes in expression of their love. This is called the Courting Festival. To seek help from a matchmaker, one must prepare 8 gifts— a basket of *zongzi*, a bag of duck eggs, a few catties of meat and noodles, and the like. A would-be son-in-law, if visiting his parents-in-law for the first time, will prepare some items used in summer—a sleeping mat, a few fans, a large gelded rooster and 10 *zongzis*. Besides the Dragon Boat Festival, the Courting Festival

端午节正式列入国家法定节日。2009年，端午节成为中国首个入选人类非物质文化遗产代表作名录的传统节日。

6. 中秋节

中秋节又称拜月节、团圆节，源于古代秋分祭月传统。为保证祭祀时呈满月状，调整到农历八月十五。中秋节定型于唐朝初年，盛行于宋朝以后。《东京梦华录》记载："中秋夜，贵家结饰台榭，民间争占酒楼玩月。"祭月、赏月、走月亮、吃月饼、玩花灯、舞龙灯、赏桂花、饮桂花酒等民俗，在美食美景中，寄托人们对美好幸福生活的追求。

中秋赏月

Admiring the Moon on the Mid-autumn Festival

also fall on the Tian Kuang Festival (Double Sixth Festival) on the 6th day of the 6th lunar month, the Mid-autumn Festival on the 15th of the 8th month, the Double Ninth Festival on the 9th day of 9th lunar month and the Winter solstice in the 11th lunar month. In 2006, the Dragon Boat Festival was put on The First National List of Intangible Cultural Heritage of China. Since 2008, the Dragon Boat Festival has been officially designated as a statutory festival. In 2009, the Dragon Boat Festival became the first Chinese traditional festival included the Representative List of Intangible Cultural Heritage of Humanity.

6. The Mid-autumn Festival

The Mid-Autumn Festival, also known as the Moon Worshipping Festival and the Reunion Festival, originated from the ancient tradition of worshipping the moon on the autumnal equinox. It was adjusted to the 15th day of the 8th lunar month to ensure a full moon during the Festival. The Mid-Autumn Festival was established in the early years of the Tang Dynasty and gained ground in the wake of the Song Dynasty. According to the *Dreams of Splendor of the Eastern Capital*, quote: "On the evening of the Mid-autumn Festival, noble families decorate their towers, pavilions and gardens, while common people scramble to occupy a space in taverns and restaurants to admire the moon." Folkways exemplified by worshipping the moon, admiring the moon, walking in the moonshine, eating mooncakes, sporting with decorated lanterns, playing dragon dances, observing sweet olives and drinking sweet olive wine, etc. in the company of delectable foods and pleasurable scenes, bespeak people's pursuit of a better and happier life. In 2006, the Mid-autumn Festival was inscribed on The First National List of Intangible Cultural Heritage of China. In 2008, the Mid-autumn Festival was designated as a statutory holiday in China.

2006年，中秋节列入首批国家级非物质文化遗产名录。2008年，中秋节被列为国家法定节假日。

7. 重阳节

重阳原指天空，九为阳数之极，天有九重，故曰重阳。汉代以九月九日为重阳，"佩茱萸，食蓬饵，饮菊华酒，令人长寿"（《西京杂记》卷三）。中原重阳习俗起于东汉上蔡。上蔡城西有伏牛山余脉冈山，又称芦岗，俗称卧龙冈。南北走向，长25千米，宽6～7千米，最高海拔98.2米，上土下石，沟壑纵横。东边是蔡国故城的宫殿区，西边是汝河故道。冈上建有蔡侯望河楼，又名看花楼。火神庙、奶奶庙、佛殿、关公庙、玉皇庙等错杂排布冈头，此地还掘出过"桓景登高处"宋代残碑一通。桓景为东汉汝南人，以仙人费长房为师。

南朝吴均《续齐谐记》载："汝南桓景随费长房游学累年，长房谓曰：'九月九日，汝家中当有灾，宜急去，令家人各作绛囊，盛茱萸以系臂，登高饮菊花酒，此祸可除。'景如言齐家登山，夕还，见鸡犬牛羊一时暴死。长房闻之曰：'此可代也。'今世人九日登高饮酒，妇人带茱萸囊，盖始于此。"

自唐中宗诏令中和、上巳、重九三天为三令节始，重阳节逐渐成为敬老节，登高成为重阳节的主题。1989年定重阳为老人节。2003年上蔡县举办了首届"中国·上蔡重阳文化节"，国家邮政局发行了一套特种邮票以纪念这个传统节日，并将邮票首发式安排在河南上蔡县举行。2005年，中国民间文艺家协会命名上蔡县为"中国重阳文化之乡"。2011年，上蔡重阳习俗列入第三批国家级非物质文化遗产名录。

7. The Double Ninth Festival

Chongyang [1] originally means the sky. "Nine" stands for the culmination of yang, and the sky has nine layers (chong), so it is called Chongyang. The 9th day of the 9th lunar month was set as the Double Ninth Festival. According to Volume 3 of the Miscellaneous Records of the Western Capital, on the Double Ninth Festival, "People wear dogwood twigs, eat pastries made from garland chrysanthemum, and drink wine brewed with chrysanthemum. This will extend people's lifespan." West of the seat of Shangcai County is a stretch of Funiu Mountains – Gang Mountain, which is also called Lugang and commonly known as Wolonggang. The mountain runs from north to south, measuring 25 kilometers long, 6-7 kilometers wide, and 98.2 meters above sea level. The upper part of the mountain is soil and lower part rocks. East of the mountain is the palatial area of the ancient city of the State of Cai, and west of the mountain is the old riverway of the Ru River. On the mountain stands the Wanghe Tower (River-watching Tower) built by Caihou, also named Kanhua Tower (Flower-watching Tower). Huoshen Temple (God of Fire Temple), Nainai Temple (Granny Temple), Buddhist halls, Temple of Lord Guan, Yuhuang Temple (Jade Emperor Temple) sprawl all over the mountain. An incomplete stele was excavated at "the site where Huan Jing ascended to a Height". Huan Jing, a local of Runan in the Eastern Han Dynasty, was apprenticed to Fei Changfang, an immortal.

In the *Continued Records on Universal Harmony* (*Xu Qi Xie Ji* in Chinese *pinyin*) by Wu Jun in the Southern Dynasties, quote "A Runan-based man named Huan Jing had been on a study tour for years with Fei Changfang, who told Huan Jing, 'On the ninth day of the ninth month, a disaster will befall your family, so you'd better leave for home right away and ask each of your family members to make a red sachet to be encased with dogwood branches and wrapped around the arm. Then they can ascend a height, drinking chrysanthemum wine, and the disaster will be eliminated.' At his teacher's advice, Huan Jing and his family climbed high up the mountain. When returning home in the evening, they found the fowls, dogs, cattle and sheep had all died. Hearing Huan Jing's words, Fei Changfang said, 'They had suffered in place of your family.' Today, the custom is

---

[1] The Double Ninth Festival is also known as the Chongyang Festival.

8. 洛阳牡丹花会

洛阳牡丹栽培始于隋，鼎盛于唐，培植有姚黄、魏紫、豆绿、赵粉等名品。欧阳修《洛阳牡丹记》，周师厚《洛阳牡丹记》《洛阳花木记》，张峋《洛阳花谱》等，记述了牡丹的栽培管理，包括择地、花性、浇灌、留蕾、防虫害、防霜冻以及嫁接、育种等栽培方法，总结出一整套较为完善的种花经验。周敦颐《爱莲说》"牡丹，花之富贵者也"，牡丹因此享有"富贵花"的称誉。现在的洛阳牡丹种植面积达10万余亩（16000英亩），有红、白、粉、黄、紫、蓝、绿、黑及复色9大色系、10种花型、1260多个品种。洛阳市有规模化牡丹观赏园12个，其中，隋唐城遗址

洛阳牡丹
Luoyang Peony

best understood as deriving from this legend of people climbing to a height while drinking wine on the 9th day of the 9th month and for women to wear sachets encased with dogwood twigs."

Since the Emperor Zhongzong of Tang decreed that the 2nd day of the 2nd lunar month, the 3rd day of the 3rd lunar month and the 9th day of the 9th lunar month be the Zhonghe Festival, the Shangsi Festival and the Double Ninth Festival, the Double Ninth Festival has evolved into a festival to show respect for the elderly. It was set as Seniors' Day in 1989. In 2003, the first "Double Ninth Cultural Festival Shangcai County, China" was held in Shangcai County, for which reason, the State Post Bureau issued a set of special postage stamps in commemoration of the traditional festival and arranged for the stamp-issuing ceremony to be held in Shangcai. China Folk Literature and Art Association named Shangcai County "Home to Chinese Double Ninth Culture". In 2011, the Double Ninth Festival custom was put on The Third National List of Intangible Cultural Heritage of China.

8. Luoyang Peony Fair

The cultivation of peony started in the Sui Dynasty and reached its heyday during the Tang Dynasty. Varieties of peony include Yao Yellow [1], Wei Purple, [2] Pea Green [3] and Zhao Pink [4]. The cultivation and management of peony, including the selection of sites, the nature of flowers, watering, bud retention, pest control, frost prevention, grafting, and seed breeding, was described in works from the *Peonies of Luoyang* Ouyang Xiu by, the *Peonies of Louyang* the *An Account of the Trees and Flowers of Luoyang* by Zhou Shihou to the *Anthography of Luoyang* by Zhang Xun, representing a complete set of the knowledge of gardening. Zhou Dunyi said in his book – *Ode to Lotus Lovers* that "The peony is the flower of rank and wealth",

---

[1] A variety of yellow cultivated by the Yao family, according to Ouyang Xiu, a famous litterateur in the Northern Song Dynasty.

[2] A variety of purple cultivated by Wei Xiang, according to Ouyang Xiu.

[3] The rarest variety with the color of pea.

[4] A variety bred by a Zhao family in the Qing Dynasty.

植物园内的千姿牡丹园是全市牡丹品种最多、花色最全、文化氛围最浓的牡丹园。公园由洛阳牡丹园、紫斑牡丹园、精品牡丹园三大园组成，是历届牡丹花会的主会场，集牡丹文化与历史文化、人文园林与自然园林为一体。中国国花园享有"中国国花第一园"之美誉，种植1080多个品种、750多亩（124英亩）、60万余株的牡丹。国家牡丹园又名中国洛阳国家牡丹基因库，是我国唯一的以国家名义命名的花卉专类园；搜集国内牡丹园艺品种600余个，野生种6个，培育新品种72个，数量50余万株，引进国外园艺品种100余个，数量5万株；年繁殖9大色系，品种齐全，花大色艳的优质商品牡丹30万株；已成为野生牡丹引种驯化、新品种培育和商品牡丹繁殖的国内最大生产基地。

1982年，牡丹花被认定为洛阳市"市花"。从1983年开始，洛阳每年四月至五月举办二十日洛阳牡丹花会。2011年，"洛阳牡丹花会"更名为"中国洛阳牡丹文化节"，并升格为国家级节会，由国家文化部和河南省人民政府主办。牡丹是洛阳的名片，中国洛阳牡丹文化节已经成为洛阳发展经济的平台和展示城市形象的窗口。

9. 开封菊花花会

开封菊花多名品，"家家菊尽黄，梁园独如霜"。唐代诗人刘禹锡的诗句道出了开封白菊之美。"梁园"位于今开封市禹王台公园。北宋刘蒙于崇宁三年（1104）著成第一部菊花专著《菊谱》，收集了35个菊花品种。开封市政府发掘菊花与城市的联系，用30年时间打造菊花节日，产生巨大的经济和文化效益。1983年，"菊花"被命名为开封市市花，并确定每年十月至十一月举办"中国开封菊花花会"。2000年，中国开封菊花花会从开封市政府主办提升为河南省人民政府主办。2009年，中国开封菊花花会被中国节庆年会评为改革开放30年"影响中国节庆产业进程的30个节庆"之一。2010年，中国风景园林学会授予开封"中国菊花名城"称号。2013年，"中国开封菊花花会"升格为国

therefore, peonies are acclaimed as "noble flowers". The peony acreage in Luoyang at present excels 16,000 acres (100 thousand Mu in Chinese), with 9 color systems (red, white, pink, yellow, purple, blue, green, black, and compound colors), 10 patterns and 1260 varieties. There are 12 large-scale ornamental gardens of peony in Luoyang City, among which, the Qianzi [1] Peony Garden in the Luoyang Sui & Tang Dynasties Relics Botanic Garden is the one with the most varieties, the most complete flower colors, and the strongest cultural atmosphere in the city. The Qianzi Peony Garden consists of Luoyang Peony Garden, Purple-spotted Peony Garden and Top Peony Garden. It is the main venue of all previous Peony Festivals, integrating peony culture and historical culture and humanistic gardens and natural gardens. The China National Flower Garden is credited as "The First Garden of China's National Flowers", with over 1,080 varieties of peonies, over 124 acres and over 600,000 peonies. The National Peony Garden, also known as the National Peony Gene Bank of Luoyang, is the only flower garden in China named after the state. It has a collection of over 500,000 peonies of 600 domestic man-cultivated varieties, 6 wild species, and 72 newly cultivated varieties. It has also introduced from abroad 50,000 peonies of over 100 varieties. Every year, over 300,000 brightly colored top-quality peonies of 9 color systems and of all kinds of varieties. Now, it has become the largest production base in China for domesticating wild peonies, cultivating new varieties, and growing commercial peonies.

The year 1982 saw the recognition of peony as the "city flower" of Luoyang. Since 1983, a 20-day long Peony Fair has been held between April and May in Luoyang. In 2011, the "Luoyang Peony Fair" was renamed "The Peony Culture Festival of Luoyang China" and upgraded to a state-level festival, co-hosted by the Ministry of Culture and the Henan Provincial Government. The festival is hosted by the Ministry of Culture and Henan Provincial Government. Peony is the name card of Luoyang, and the Peony Culture Festival of Luoyang China has become a platform for economic development and a window for the city's image.

9. Kaifeng Chrysanthemum Fair

There are many famous styles of Kaifeng chrysanthemums. Liu Yuxi, a poet in

---

[1] Qianzi means various types and patterns.

家级节会，更名为"中国开封菊花文化节"，由国家住建部和河南省人民政府主办。今天的中国开封菊花文化节已经成为一个融赏花观灯、旅游观光、经贸合作与文化交流为一体的大型综合性经济文化活动节日，一个月长的会期，将开封装点成菊花海洋，吸引着世界人民爱美的目光。

开封菊花展
Kaifeng Chrysanthemum Exhibition

the Tang Dynasty gave full expression to the beauty of Kaifeng chrysanthemums in a line in his poem, which describes "The chrysanthemums of every household are yellow, only those of the Liang Garden frost-white." The Liang garden is seated in the Yuwangtai Park in Kaifeng. In 1104, Liu Meng, living in the Northern Song Dynasty, wrote the first monograph on chrysanthemums – *Anthography of Chrysanthemums*, which described 35 varieties. The government of Kaifeng City explored the connection between chrysanthemums and the city, spending 30 years setting up a chrysanthemum festival, which has brought huge economic and cultural benefits. In 1983, "Chrysanthemum" was officially designated as the city flower of Kaifeng, and a decision was made that "The Chrysanthemum Fair of Kaifeng, China" would be held from October to November every year. In 2000, the hosting of the Chrysanthemum Fair of Kaifeng, China was shifted from the government of Kaifeng City to the Henan Provincial Government. In 2009, the Chrysanthemum Fair of Kaifeng, China was awarded by the China Festivals Association as one of the "30 Festivals Influencing the Progress of China's Festival Industry". In 2010, Kaifeng was awarded the title of "The Famous City of Chrysanthemums in China" by the Chinese Society of Landscape Architecture. In 2013, the "Chrysanthemum Fair of Kaifeng, China" was elevated to a national festival and renamed "The Chrysanthemum Culture Festival of Kaifeng, China", co-hosted by the Ministry of Housing and Urban-rural Development and the Henan provincial government. The present Chrysanthemum Culture Festival of Kaifeng, China has become a hugely inclusive festival for cultural and economic events that combines flower viewing, lantern watching, touring, economic and trade cooperation and cultural exchanges. The month-long festival will adorn Kaifeng into an ocean of chrysanthemums, catching the beauty-oriented eyes of people around the world.

第二章

中原庙会

Chapter 2

Temple Fairs in the Central Plains

中原历史悠久，民俗底蕴深厚，而庙会则堪称是中原民俗的博览会，中原庙会渗透着中原民众的多元信仰和千姿百态的民俗艺术。庙会因多在祭祀神灵的日子在寺庙附近举行而得名。早期庙会起源于拜神活动，后与农时贸易相结合，成为兼具拜神、娱乐、贸易、会客等多种功能的民间传统集市。河南庙会突出特点是产生年代久远，保存着许多古老的神话、信仰和民俗，是中国传统文化的"活化石"。河南涉及中华始祖的庙会就有盘古、伏羲、女娲、炎帝、黄帝、大禹等，这与中原地区是中华文明起源的重要发祥地是分不开的，不少人文始祖都在此留下了浓墨重彩的一笔。

中原庙会形式多样，依据不同标准有不同分类。从地域划分来看，有学者将中原庙会划分为五大片区：豫中以郑州和开封为中心，以郑州城隍庙会和开封春节庙会为代表；豫西以中岳嵩山庙会和洛阳庙会为代表；豫东以周口淮阳太昊陵庙会最为盛大；豫北以太行山区浚县庙会最

开封春节万岁山庙会
Kaifeng Wansuishan Temple Fair during the Spring Festival

Chapter 2 Temple Fairs in the Central Plains

The Central Plains enjoy a long history and a profound folklore heritage, while temple fairs can be called folklore expositions of the Central Plains. The Central Plains temple fairs are imbued with the Central Plains people's diverse faiths multifarious folklore arts. The temple fair got its name because it is generally held near temples on the god-worshipping days. Early temple fairs originated from the worship of gods, and later, when combined with agricultural trade, became traditional folk markets featuring various functions such as worshipping, entertaining, trading, and meeting friends. The prominent feature of Henan temple fairs is that they emerged a long time ago and preserve many ancient myths, beliefs, and customs, so they are called the "Living fossils" of traditional Chinese culture. The temple fairs relating to the ancestors of the China include Pangu, Fuxi, Nüwa, The Yan Emperor, the Yellow Emperor, Yu the Great, and the like. This is closely associated with the fact that region of the Central Plains is an important birthplace of the Chinese civilization, where many ancient litterateurs have left their remarkable works.

The temple fairs of the Central Plains take on different forms and have various classifications in light different criteria. Geographically, some scholars have classified the Central Plains temple fairs into five major areas. First, in Zhengzhou City and Kaifeng City that are the area of Central Henan, the representative temple fairs are Zhengzhou Chenghuang Temple Fair and Kaifeng Spring Festival Temple Fair. Second, in western Henan, the typical temple fairs are the Central Mountain – Mount Song Temple Fair and the Luoyang Temple Fair. Third, in eastern Henan, the grandest temple fair is the Taihao Mausoleum Fair in Huaiyang County, Zhoukou City. Fourth, in northern Henan, the most famous temple fair is the Xun County Temple Fair in Taihang Mountains. Fifth, in southern Henan, there are more rural temple fairs, because it was influenced by the Chu Culture in history.

The Central Plains temple fairs can also be categorized according to what are worshipped. First, the temple fairs springing from Buddhist temples account for the most in the Central Plains, such as the Xiangguo Temple Fair in Kaifeng and the Baima Temple (also named White Horse Temple) Fair in Luoyang. Second, the temple fairs include strong Taoist atmospheres, like the Laojuntai Temple Fair in Luyi County that was set up to worship Laozi, the founder of Taoism,

为著名；豫南多乡村庙会，历史上受楚文化影响。

中原庙会按照祭祀对象又可以分为不同类别。一是因佛教寺庙而兴起的庙会，这类庙会在中原地区众多，著名的有开封相国寺庙会、洛阳白马寺庙会等；二是道教色彩浓厚的庙会，如鹿邑老君台庙会是为了祭祀道家创始人老子，此外还有玉皇庙会、王母娘娘庙会等；三是除了佛教和道教之外，中原还有不少传承久远的神话和历史人物的庙会，承载着祖先崇拜的观念，也富有文化教育意义，这类庙会著名的有淮阳太昊伏羲庙会、西华女娲庙会、桐柏盘古庙会、新郑黄帝祭祀大典、汤阴岳飞庙会、关帝庙会等；四是中原庙会中还有对自然崇拜而兴起的庙会，如对黄河和济河崇拜而兴起的河渎庙会，因土地崇拜而诞生的土地庙会，祈求风调雨顺而兴起的龙王庙会，因节气时令而兴的谷雨会等。

中原庙会的首要功能是祭祀神灵，人们多祈求满足现世的愿望。中原地区的民间信仰存在信仰杂糅和实用功利性，烧香祭拜多祈求现世的财运、家人平安、子孙、姻缘、升学等，常用"心诚则灵"来安慰自己。"多子多福"是中原民众传承几千年的观念，这与农业社会需要大量劳动力密不可分，而今河南户籍人口已经超过1亿人，与这一传统观念不无关系。中原传统上以农耕为主要生计方式，对于气候十分关注，农民期盼风调雨顺，所以不少庙会保留着求雨习俗。

中原庙会娱乐活动丰富多彩，包括河南地方戏的演出、社火和其他各种民间文艺等。传统庙会上为了娱神常会请戏班来演唱"拿手戏"，多为河南地方特色的豫剧、曲剧等曲目，在戏台上演出，锣鼓喧天，下面观众人山人海，有时连唱几天，称为"唱大戏"。庙会社火形式多样，如踩高跷、舞狮子、舞龙、划旱船、擂大鼓、担经挑等。

庙会的祭神和娱乐活动引来了大量人流，便有了商贸活动。当地农民会将地方上的特产和自家的禽蛋、手工艺品等拿出来出售，还会有各色地方美食。前来赶会的人们，除了祭神、娱乐和商品贸易，也会借此走亲访友，拜访庙会附近村子的亲戚朋友，联络感情，礼尚往来。因此，

in addition to the Jade Emperor Temple Fair and the Queen Mother of the West Temple Fair. Third, in addition to the temple fairs associated with Buddhism and Taoism, there are also many temple fairs relating to longstanding myths and historical figures in the Central Plains, which suggest the concept of ancestral worship and are of cultural and educational significance, represented by the Taihao Fuxi Temple Fair in Huaiyang District, the Nüwa Temple Fair in Xihua County, the Pangu Temple Fair in Tongbai County, the Yellow Emperor Worshipping Ceremony, the Yue Fei Temple Fair in Tangyin County and Temple of Lord Guan Fair. Fourth, there are also the Hedu Temple Fair growing out of worship of the Yellow River and the Ji River, the God of the Land Temple Fair originating from worship of land, the Dragon King Temple Fair where people pray for agreeable winds and timely rains, and the Grain Rain Fair originating from solar terms and seasons and so on.

The primary function of the Central Plains temple fair is to worship gods. On those occasions, people typically pray for the fulfillment of their wishes in this life. The folk faiths in the Central Plains area feature mixed faiths and utilitarianism. People, when making sacrificial offerings and burning incense, mostly pray for fortune in their present life, for the safety of their families, for their offspring, for marriage and for getting into a higher educational institution. They often use the phrase "Sincerity makes your prayer work" as a comfort. The belief of "More sons bring more fortune" has been passed down and carried forward for thousands of years in the Central Plains, a result of the need for a large amount of labor force in an agrarian society. The registered population of Henan excels 0.1 billion, which to a certain degree is related to the belief. Farming is the main means of livelihood in the Central Plains, so the climate is of great concern to farmers, who expect agreeable winds and timely rains. The custom of praying for rain is still practiced at many temple fairs.

There are many entertainments at the temple fairs in the Central Plains, including performances of Henan local operas, Shehuo and other folk arts. To please the gods, traditional temple fairs often invite opera troupes to perform their "Masterpieces", most of which are distinctive Henan opera, Quju opera and other items. When the opera is performed on the stage, the drums and gongs rumble, and the audience throngs around. Sometimes, the opera is performed for days in a row, or what is known as to "Put on a big show". The Shehuo at temple fairs is performed in different forms, such as stilt walking, lion dancing, dragon dancing,

庙会可以说是沟通人与人、人与神之间感情的重要桥梁。

1. 淮阳庙会

淮阳太昊陵庙会从中国农历二月二一直到三月三，持续一个月时间，是为祭拜太昊伏羲而兴起的庙会。太昊陵庙会，历史之久，规模之大，会期之长，人数之多，居豫东庙会之首。太昊陵庙会时前来赶庙会的人群绵延数里，曾在 2008 年人流高峰时统计一天就有 82 万人前来参加，一举打破了吉尼斯世界纪录。

太昊陵庙会的起源相传和中华始祖伏羲女娲有关。当地有神话传说，相传很久以前村子里生活着伏羲和女娲兄妹，他们偶然间救助了一只白龟，经常给其粮食吃。一天白龟告诉兄妹二人，要天塌地陷了，让他们

淮阳庙会
Huaiyang Temple Fair

land boat dancing, drum beating, and pole-carrying dancing, etc. God worshipping entertainments at temple fairs attract many people, and trade and commerce ensue. Local farmers sell local specialties, fowls, eggs, and handicrafts. Various kinds of local food are also served. Fairgoers, besides worshiping the gods, engaging in entertainment, and trading goods, also take this opportunity to visit friends and relatives in the villages nearby, strengthening their connections and returning the favors they received before. Temple fairs, therefore, serve as an important bridge between people and people, and between people and the gods.

1. Huaiyang Temple Fair

The Taihao Mausoleum Temple Fair in Huaiyang District, a fair that emerged for worshipping Taihao Fuxi, lasts one month from the 2nd day of the 2nd month to the 3rd day of the 3rd month. The Fair tops all other temple fairs in Eastern Henan in terms of history, scale, duration, and the number of fairgoers. The throng of the fairgoers at the Taihao Mausoleum Temple Fair stretches for miles. At the fairgoer flow peak in 2008, there were 820,000 people coming to attend the Fair in only one day, breaking the Guinness World Record.

Legend has it that the origin of the Fair stems from Fuxi and Nüwa, the ancestors of the Chinese nation. According to the local myth, there once lived in the village Fuxi, the brother, and Nüwa, the sister, who rescued a white turtle by chance and often fed it. One day, the white turtle told the two siblings that the sky was to collapse and the earth was about to sink. The turtle suggested that the siblings take shelter in its stomach. Following its advice, the two siblings got into the white turtle's stomach, in which they found the food previously given to the turtle. They fed on the food and waited inside until everything settled outside. When getting out, they found that there was a big hole in the sky, and no one was on the earth. The brother and sister, after mending the sky, let two millstones roll down two mountains to decide if they should get married. The rolling millstones ended up fitting into each other, so the brother and sister tied the knot, and made earth into men. Humans prosper once again. Fuxi and Nüwa made fishing nets and taught people to fish and prescribed the rites for marriage. The local people label Fuxi as Master Primogenitor and Nüwa as Girl Primogenitor, and they come to make a sacrifice in the second lunar month every year. This is how the Taihao

躲进自己的肚子里避难。兄妹二人听从了，进白龟肚子里以后发现了以前送给它的粮食，以此充饥，等外面安定之后才出来，发现天上破了一个大洞，地上没有了人烟。兄妹二人就将天补好，然后从两山上各自滚下磨盘来决定是否成亲，结果磨盘竟然合在了一起，兄妹成亲，后抟土造人，人类才又兴旺了起来。伏羲和女娲又制作了渔网教人们捕鱼，规定了嫁娶的礼仪。当地将伏羲、女娲称为人祖爷和人祖姑娘，每年二月份都要来祭拜，由此有了太昊陵庙会。

庙会期间，人们从四面八方赶来，商贩们也各自忙碌着支起摊位，摆上琳琅的商品，一派繁华的庙会场景。太昊陵庙会上人山人海，除了民间的贸易行为、娱乐活动之外，最为突出的是求子习俗与其所呈现的生育文化。求子仪式主要有拴娃娃、摸子孙窑、献旗杆和担经挑、请泥泥狗和布老虎等。

在淮阳古庙会上，随处可以看到可爱的布老虎和各种造型的泥泥狗，一般去庙会的人都会买泥泥狗和布老虎。庙会期间，沿路的孩子可以拦路向去参加庙会的人索要泥泥狗，并唱起歌谣："老斋公，慢慢走，给把泥泥狗，您老活到九十九。"不论走到哪里，碰到向你要泥泥狗的孩子，你都要赶快把它撒在地上，让孩子们拾，你趁机跑掉。因为把"泥泥狗"送给儿童或亲友，可以使人消灾祛病，吉祥平安。淮阳泥泥狗被誉为原始生殖崇拜文化的活化石，其造型有双头狗、双头猴、虎拉猴、猴骑狗等，有600多种不同造型，常见的有100多种传统造型。

在淮阳人祖庙会上，还时常有三五成群的妇女担着花篮在统天殿前或陵墓前唱耍，群众称其为"担花篮"。流行于太昊陵进香会上的担经挑是原始社会以舞祭媒保留下来的一种遗俗，集祭祖、娱神、求子为一体。太昊陵庙会是当地极富有民俗色彩的重要活动，庙会上各种祭祀活动不一而足，不仅仅局限于上述描写的活动，还有其他表现形式。

Mausoleum Temple Fair came to pass.

During the temple fair, people race to the site from all sides, while peddlers are busy setting up stalls with a wide variety of goods, making it a bustling scene. Apart from unofficial trade and entertainment, the most striking part of the fair is the children-seeking custom and the birth-giving culture it presents. The rituals of seeking children mainly include Tying Clay Babies, Feeling the Offspring Cave, Presenting the Flagpole, Pole-carrying Dancing and Inviting Clay Dogs and Cloth Tigers, etc.

At the ancient temple fair in Huaiyang, attractive cloth tigers and differently shaped clay dogs are seen everywhere, and generally, the fairgoers will buy clay dogs and cloth tigers. During the temple fair, children along the way can stop the fairgoers and ask them for clay dogs. They sing a song whose lyrics read: "Master, please walk slowly, give me a pack of clay dogs, and you will live up to 99." Wherever you go, when meeting children asking for clay dogs, you should quickly scatter them on the ground and let the children pick them up, then you can take the chance to run away. Giving the "clay dogs" to children or relatives and friends can help to remove disasters and diseases and get luck and peace. Clay dogs of Huaiyang are regarded as a living fossil of primitive fertility worship culture. They have different shapes—two-headed dogs, two-headed monkeys, tiger-pulled monkeys, and monkey-ridden dogs etc. There are more than 100 common traditional shapes out of a total of over 600 different shapes.

At Huaiyang People's Ancestral Temple Fairs, groups of women carrying flower baskets are often seen singing in front of the Tongtian Hall or in front of the Taihao Mausoleum, which is called "Carrying Flower Baskets". Pole-carrying dancing that is popular at the Joss Sticks Offering Fair at the Taihao Mausoleum is a relic of the primitive society, which integrates sacrificing to ancestors, pleasing the gods, and seeking offspring. The Temple Fair at the Taihao Mausoleum is an important event fully displaying the folkways. There are various kinds of worshipping activities at the fair, not only the activities described above, but also activities in other forms.

2. 新郑黄帝故里拜祖大典

据史料记载，河南新郑是中华人文始祖轩辕黄帝的诞生地、建都地。距今7000～8000年的裴李岗文化就产生于此，并发掘出中国现存最早的石磨盘和磨棒，代表当时农业的发展水平；5000年前文明始祖黄帝在此建都，统一诸多部落，制舟车、筑宫室、创音律、养桑蚕等，开辟了华夏文明新纪元；2000多年前，春秋战国时期郑国和韩国分别在此建都，逐鹿中原，留下多少惊心动魄的历史故事。每年阳春三月三，新郑祭祀黄帝的仪式从古至今绵延不绝，现在形成了具有地方特色和海内外广泛影响力的拜祖大典，并被列入国家级非物质文化遗产保护名录。

在民间有"三月三，拜轩辕"的说法，相传这一天是轩辕黄帝的诞生日，公祭和民间祭祀有所不同。公祭主要是官方祭拜，有严格仪式流程，规模宏大，参与祭拜的人员地位较高，是有组织的集体性活动。明清时期祭拜黄帝的仪式就十分隆重，而今在黄帝故里广场每年都会举行全球直播的拜祖大典，以吸引海内外同胞对中华始祖的认同感，增强中华民族的凝聚力。公拜的人员一般是主办、承办单位主要领导和社会各界代表，并邀请国家和其他省区、地市有关领导以及海外华人、华裔、

新郑黄帝故里拜祖大典
The Xinzheng Yellow Emperor Worship Ceremony

2. The Xinzheng Yellow Emperor Worship Ceremony

According to the historical records, Xinzheng in Henan Province is the birthplace and capital of Xuanyuan Yellow Emperor, the first ancestor of Chinese culture. Peiligang Culture came into being here 7000 to 8000 years ago. The earliest stone grinding plates and rods in China were excavated here, representing the development level of agriculture at that time. Five thousand years ago, the ancestor of civilization, Yellow Emperor, established the capital here, unified many tribes, made boats, built palaces, created music, and raised silkworms, opening a new era of Chinese civilization. More than 2,000 years ago, the State of Zheng and Han respectively established their capitals here during the Spring and Autumn Period and the Warring States Period and fought in the Central Plains, leaving many thrilling historical stories. Every year on the third day of the third lunar month, the grand ceremony to worship the Yellow Emperor in Xinzheng has been going on from ancient times to the present. It has become an ancestor worship ceremony with local characteristics and extensive influence at home and abroad, and has been listed in the National Intangible Cultural Heritage protection list.

There is a folk saying that it is the day for people to "worship Xuanyuan on the third day of the third lunar month". It is said that Xuanyuan Yellow Emperor was born on this day. The public sacrifice is different from the folk sacrifice. The public sacrifice is mainly an official sacrifice, with strict ritual procedures and usually a large scale. Personnel who participated in the sacrifice have a high status. It is an organized collective activity. In the Ming and Qing Dynasties, the worship ceremony was very grand. Now, a globally broadcast Ancestor Worship Ceremony will be held every year in the square of the hometown of the Yellow Emperor which aims at attracting compatriots home and abroad to identify with the Chinese ancestors and enhance the cohesion of the Chinese nation. The public worship personnel are generally the main leaders of the host units and sponsoring units and representatives from all walks of life. The relevant leaders of the state and other provinces, regions and cities, as well as representatives of overseas Chinese, ethnic Chinese, and surname clan associations are invited to participate. The grand ceremony proceeded in a solemn atmosphere following 9 established procedures: a 21-gun salute, the speech of the person in charge of the organizer, the offering of

姓氏宗亲会代表参加。仪式主要流程有九项，包括全体肃立鸣炮 21 响、承办单位主要负责人致辞、领导敬献花篮、上香、吟唱《黄帝颂》、恭读《黄帝文》、全体行祭拜礼、乐舞敬拜、敬奉黄河水等流程。参与人员达数千人，整个场面庄严肃穆，恢宏壮观。

而民间的黄帝祭祀则更多民俗色彩，是民众自发形成的，传承久远，约定俗成，没有固定成文的仪式流程和制度。每年三月三，在轩辕黄帝故里和始祖山（具茨山）两处都有周边市县的民众前来祭拜，依照传统习俗，要焚香上供，或祈求保佑，或祈求雨水，或答谢还愿。本地民众多以村为单位，或以庙会形式出现，拜祖队伍少则几十人，多则几百人，前面由会首或主持人举着令旗，接着是多面大锣引领开道，后面是八面牌和两红两黄四顶大伞，后面紧跟着的是青龙、黄龙、狮子舞等民间社火，接下来是铜器乐队。最后拜祖的村民抬着全猪、羊、水果、糕点等供品和香裱等祭品，队伍浩浩荡荡，一路井然有序，表示对黄帝始祖的尊敬。主持人摆上供品，上香，跪拜三叩首，然后肃立祈祷，民众也行叩拜礼。祭拜后开始燃放鞭炮，龙狮舞动，乐器齐鸣，娱乐始祖。香客们开始自行焚香祈祷，说出自己祈求的事情。此外，民间还有三月三上具茨山采药、求药习俗，认为这天所采药材有特殊功效，这与黄帝被认为是中医的最早发明者有关。

关于黄帝有诸多神话传说，能够体现其超凡的文治武功。总体来看，黄帝是一个"箭垛式"人物，兼具神性和人性，是早期先民不断开拓进取、自强不息、走向民族融合的象征。对黄帝的祭拜是对中华民族人文始祖的崇敬和伟大精神的弘扬。

flower baskets, burning incense, singing *The Yellow Emperor Odes*, reading *The Lines* of *Worshipping the Yellow Emperor*, dancing and honoring the water of the Yellow River and so on. There were thousands of participants.

    The folk sacrifice is more of folk custom. It is formed spontaneously by the people and has been inherited for a long time. There is no fixed written ritual process and system. On the third day of the third lunar month every year, people from nearby cities and counties come to worship at the hometown of the Yellow Emperor Xuanyuan and the Shizu Mountain (Juci Mountain). According to the traditional customs, people burn incense to offer sacrifices, pray for blessings, pray for rain, or repay their wishes. Most of the local people take the village as a unit or take the form of a temple fair. In the front, the leader or host holds the flag, followed by many big gongs to lead the way. It is an eight-faced card, two red, two yellow and four big umbrellas, followed by Qinglong, Huanglong, and Lion Dance and then a bronze band. The villagers who worshipped their ancestors last carried the whole pigs, sheep, fruits, cakes etc. and other offerings and incense framed sacrifices. The team was orderly, showing their respect for the ancestor of the Yellow Emperor. The host offered sacrifices, burnt incense, knelt down three times, then stood up to pray, and the other people also kowtowed. After the sacrifice, people began to set off firecrackers, play musical instruments, and entertain the ancestors. The pilgrims began to burn incense and pray by themselves, saying what they prayed for. In addition, there is a folk custom of collecting and seeking medicine on the third day of the third lunar month. It is believed that the medicinal materials collected on that day have special effects, which is related to the fact that the Yellow Emperor is considered to be the earliest inventor of Traditional Chinese Medicine.

    There are many myths and legends about the Yellow Emperor, which can reflect his extraordinary arts and military skills. Generally speaking, the Yellow

3. 商丘火神台庙会

商丘火神台庙会以祭拜火神而闻名天下，火神台又名"火星台""阏伯台"，位于河南东部商丘市区内。每年的正月初七、四月初四、六月二十三日，附近各县市的数万人前来参加庙会，远及周边山东、安徽、江苏、河北等地的民众，尤其以正月初七最盛。火神台祭祀的主神为阏伯，当地称为"火神爷"，相传他是三皇五帝中"高辛氏帝喾"的儿子，在此主持星辰祭祀，并保存火种。这里流传着和古希腊神话中普罗米修斯盗圣火一样悲壮的神话故事。其背后隐含的是人类早期对火的崇拜，人们在商丘这个地方崇拜火神阏伯，而这个地方对应天上大火星所在的区域，所以商丘火神台庙会反映了早期先民对发明使用火和天上大火星的崇拜，后来人们每逢春节祭灶等也与火神信仰密切相关。至今在豫东地区还流传着与阏伯火神信仰相关的习俗。

庙会期间的传统民俗活动有很多。人们会将家乡带来的土带过来，堆在火神台上，借此表达自己对火神阏伯的敬意。而火神台上的草木都被认为赋予了灵性，在庙会期间会有人来请"药"，带回去一些用水煮了给生病的人喝了被认为能够治病。人们还来烧香、上供，有许多民间

商丘火神台庙会
Shangqiu Huoshentai Temple Fair

Emperor was an "arrow-target" figure [1], with both divinity and humanity. It was a symbol of the early ancestors' continuous pioneering, self-improvement and national integration. Worshiping the Yellow Emperor is the admiration and promotion of the great spirit of the humanistic ancestor of the Chinese nation.

3. Shangqiu Huoshentai Temple Fair

Shangqiu Huoshentai Temple Fair is famous for worshipping the God of fire. Huoshentai, also known as "Huoxingtai" or "Ebotai", is located in Shangqiu City, which is in the eastern part of Henan province. Every year on the seventh day of the first lunar month, the fourth day of the fourth lunar month, and the 23rd day of the sixth lunar month, tens of thousands of people from nearby counties and cities come to participate in the temple fair, as well as people from Shandong, Anhui, Jiangsu, Hebei and other places, especially on the seventh day of the first lunar month. The main deity sacrificed at the Huoshentai is E Bo, locally known as "Huoshenye". It is said that he is the son of the "Gaoxin Emperor" among the three emperors and five emperors. He presides over the star sacrifice here and preserves the fire. There is a mythical story as tragic as Prometheus stealing the holy flame in ancient Greek mythology. Behind it is the worship of fire of human beings in the early days. People worship the God of fire in Shangqiu, and Shangqiu corresponds to the area where the Mars in the sky is located. Therefore, Shangqiu Huoshentai Temple Fair reflects the worship of the early ancestors for the invention and use of fire and the Mars in the sky. Later, people worship the kitchen in the Spring Festival, etc. which is closely related to the belief of the God of fire. There are still customs related to the fire God belief of E Bo in the east of Henan Province.

There are many traditional folk activities during the temple fair. People will bring the soil from their hometown and pile it on Huoshentai to express their

---

[1] During the development of folk literature, people often take some well-known characters as protagonists, constantly weave various legends and stories, and constantly absorb various scattered legends and story plots so that the legends with these characters as protagonists gradually expand and develop like snowballs. The protagonists are called arrow-target figures.

自发组织的香火会。火神会最热闹的活动是"火龙舞",在震天的锣鼓声中,一条巨大的火龙被几个壮汉一声吆喝舞起来,龙口中吐出焰火,龙身和龙尾装着花炮,噼啪乱响,火光四射,大家一起喊着号子,让火龙飞舞盘旋,直冲云霄,引来观众阵阵喝彩。人们相信舞火龙能够娱乐火神,保佑人们免受火灾,而又能使生活变得红红火火,既热闹,又具有了象征意义。此外,庙会期间还有踩高跷、肘阁、划旱船、唱大戏等民间文艺活动。

4. 宝丰马街书会

"中国听书哪里去,河南马街等着你。"河南宝丰县城南的马街村,因每年正月期间举行的规模宏大的庙会和书会而闻名于世。马街书会在正月十三达到高潮,所以又称为"十三马街会",书会兴盛时有几百台民间曲艺、数千名民间艺术家在同时演出,堪称是"中国民间的百老汇"。2006年,马街书会列入了第一批国家级非物质文化遗产。根据当地火神庙碑文记载,马街书会距今已有700余年的历史,而在清朝后期达到高潮,当时采用统计人数的方法十分巧妙,凡来参会的民间艺人向火神庙进一枚铜钱作为香火钱,而其他人则不能敬献铜钱,在正月书会期间共收到2700枚铜钱,相当于2700位艺人来参会演出。

关于马街书会的诞生,当地有不少传说。一种说法是东汉前,王莽撵刘秀至马街村东的应河岸边,时日正月十三,正在火神庙祭祀的乡民艺人纷纷相助汉军竞渡,阻击莽军追兵。刘秀当了皇帝后,降旨免去马街一带三年皇粮,钦赐"三皇社"御牌一面,后来这里的人便以救驾之日为会期,年年起会,感谢皇恩。至今当地仍有"光武封、书会兴"的说法。还有一说是早年马街有一位叫马德平的老说书艺人,教出了很多弟子,每年正月十三,弟子们从四面八方赶来为其献艺祝寿。这样年复一年,渐渐成了书会传统。

马街书会上艺人众多,曲目繁多,百花齐放,有河南坠子、湖北渔

respect for E Bo. The plants and trees there are believed to be endowed with spirituality. During the temple fair, people will come to ask for medicine and bring back some boiled water to the sick people to drink, which is considered to be able to cure the disease. People also come to burn incense and offer offerings, and there are many incense parties organized by the people. The most lively activity is Fire Dragon Dance. A huge fire dragon was danced by several strong men among the thundering sound of gongs and drums. Fireworks spit out from the dragon's mouth, and the dragon's body and tail were equipped with firecrackers, which crackled and blazed in all directions. Everyone chanted horns together, making the fire dragon fly and circle into the sky, attracting bursts of applause from the audience. People believe that the dragon dance can entertain the god of fire, protect people from fire, and make life prosperous. In addition, during the temple fair, there are also folk cultural activities such as walking on stilts, elbow pavilions, paddling boats, and singing operas.

4. Majie Folk Arts [1] Fair in Baofeng County

Majie is a good place for people to enjoy all kinds of folk musical art. Majie Village in the south of Baofeng County, Henan Province, is famous for the large-scale temple fair and Majie Folk Arts Fair held during the first month of each year. It reaches its climax on the 13th day of the first month, so it is also called "The 13th Story Telling Fair". During the times of prosperity, there were hundreds and thousands of folk artists performing at the same time, which can be called "The Broadway of Chinese Folk". In 2006, it was included in the first batch of national intangible cultural heritage. According to the inscriptions of the local fire temple, Majie Folk Arts Fair has a history of more than 700 years, and reached its climax in the late Qing Dynasty. At that time, the method of counting the number of people was very clever. All the folk artists who came to the fair put a copper coin into the fire temple as incense money, while other people are not allowed to offer copper coins. During the first month, a total of 2700 copper coins were received, which was equivalent to 2700 artists to participate in the performance.

---

[1] Folk Arts refer to folk vocal arts such as ballad singing, story-telling, comic dialogue, clapper talk and crosstalk.

宝丰马街书会
Majie Folk Arts Fair in Baofeng County

鼓、四川清音、山东琴书、凤阳花鼓、上海平话、徐州琴书、三弦书、大鼓书、评书、乱弹、道情等。其中河南坠子是书会第一大曲种，常用一个叫作"简板"的乐器来伴奏，宽约3厘米，长30到40厘米。此外，还有二胡、古琴、木鱼、唢呐等伴奏乐器。

  艺人在书会上说唱称为"亮书"，邀请艺人说唱称为"写书"。亮书是艺人们在正月十三这天争先恐后抢占有利地点，称为"占摊儿"，他们在盛大的书会会场上摆阵打擂，尽情展现自己的才艺，要拿出自己的压箱底绝活来吸引观众。喝彩声越高说明越得到观众青睐，赢得了好名声，后续才能被更多人以更高价格请到家里去表演。

  在艺人们"亮书"之后，"写书人"便因元宵灯会、结婚、寿宴等邀请艺人们去家里表演。而邀请艺人去说书前，当地主人家会耐心听众多艺人们的演唱，比较他们的风格和水平，选出最为中意的"写书"对象，写书时说明自己的住处和来意，进行讨价还价，或者耳语，或者打

There are many local legends about the birth of Majie Folk Arts Fair. One theory is that before the Eastern Han Dynasty, Wang Mang chased Liu Xiu to the bank of the Yinghe River in the east of Majie Village. On the 13th day of the first lunar month, local artists who were sacrificing at the Huoshen Temple helped the Han Army and stopped the pursuit of the Mang army. After Liu Xiu became emperor, he made a decree to exempt the three-year imperial grain in Majie and granted the Royal token of "Sanhuang society". Later, the people there took the day of rescue as the meeting period and began to meet every year to thank the emperor for his kindness. Nowadays, there is still a saying in the local area that "Once Liu Xiu was crowned emperor, Majie Folk Arts Fair flourished". Another story is that in the early years, there was an old storyteller named Ma Deping in Majie, who had many disciples. On the 13th day of the first lunar month of each year, his disciples converged on Majie to celebrate his birthday. Year after year, it has become a tradition of Majie Folk Arts Fair.

At Majie Folk Arts Fair, there are many artists with a wide variety of repertoires, including Henan Zhuizi, Hubei Yugu, Sichuan Qingyin, Shandong Qinshu, Fengyang Huagu, Shanghai Pinghua, Xuzhou Qinshu, Sanxianshu, Dagushu, Storytelling, Random play, Daoqing, etc. Henan Zhuizi is the largest one. It is often accompanied by a percussion instrument called "Jianban" which is about 3cm wide and 30-40cm long. In addition, there are accompaniment instruments such as Erhu, Guqin, Muyu and Suona, and so on.

The story telling and opera singing at Majie Folk Arts Fair is called "Liangshu"and inviting artists to tell stories and sing is called "Xieshu". On the 13th day of the first month of the lunar calendar, artists scramble to seize a favorable place, which is called "Occupying stalls". They set up a challenge in the grand fair to show their talents to the fullest and try their best to attract the audience. The louder the applause, the more popular they are with the audience. Only after winning a good reputation will they be invited to home by more people to perform at a higher price.

After the artists perform, people will invite them to perform at home for the Lantern Festival, marriage, birthday banquet and so on. Before inviting artists to tell stories, the hosts listen to the singing of many artists patiently, compare their styles and levels, select the favorite one, explain their residence and purpose,

手势。正月十三、十四、十五、十六被请走的艺人说明演唱得到了民众的认可，而之后几天被请走的艺人水平则打了折扣。在书会上获得报酬最高的艺人，就成为当年的书状元，被艺人们所羡慕，获得了极大认可。马街书会是民间文艺的"百老汇"，是生生不息的民间艺术奇花，反映出中原人的多彩面貌，歌颂着中国人的真善美。

and bargain through whisper or sign. The artists invited before the 13th, 14th, 15th, and 16th of the first lunar month are recognized by the public, while those invited after are not. The artist who receives the highest remuneration is the top artist of the year. He will be admired and greatly recognized. Majie Folk Arts Fair is a "Broadway" of folk literature and art. It is an ever-growing folk art wonder, reflecting the colorful life of the people in the Central Plains and praising the truth, goodness and beauty of the Chinese people.

第三章

人生礼仪

Chapter 3

Rites

第三章 人生礼仪

中国被称为"礼仪之邦",早在先秦时期就形成了礼乐教化的观念,有专门阐述礼仪的《礼记》《仪礼》《周礼》等著作传世。"知书达礼"是中国传统社会的做人追求。在中原地区,礼乐文化源远流长,周公营洛邑(今洛阳)、制礼乐。在中原地区,礼乐文化由上层贵族逐渐下沉到民间,与民间日常生活中的人生礼仪相结合,形成了礼俗互动的局面。中原地区强调"礼尚往来",对重要的人生礼仪尤为重视。生子、结婚、丧葬等是人生中的重要大事,不仅关系到个体成长,还关乎家族兴衰、传宗接代,所以产生了丰富、繁多的礼俗仪式。中原地区依据人生仪礼举行的目的和崇尚颜色不同,划分为"红事"和"白事",红事主要指一些喜庆热闹的礼仪,包括婚礼、诞生礼、寿礼等,崇尚红色喜庆色调;而白事主要是指葬礼,以肃穆圣洁的白色为仪式主色调。

一、生育仪式

生儿育女在中原地区从古至今备受重视,青年夫妻刚结婚收到的贺词往往是"新婚快乐,早生贵子",结婚后来年生个大胖娃娃是所有喜婆婆的心愿。河南民间从婚后求子、怀孕到婴儿降生和养育成长,形成了一整套风俗,显示出对生命的呵护与尊重。

1. 求子

在原始社会时期,人们还未认识生育是两性结合的结果,将怀孕视为是人神感应或神灵赐予。在民间流传着诸多感孕而生的神话,如踩着巨人足迹而生的周代祖先后稷,吃了鸟卵而生的商代祖先契等,以至于到了封建社会帝王为了神化其出生而造出了感龙而生、感星象而生等神话。在民间则流传着向神灵求子的习俗,尤其对婚后一直不育的夫妻是一种慰藉。

在中原地区民众求子时祭拜的神灵诸多,常拜的有送子娘娘、子孙

China is known as the "Land of rites and ceremonies". As early as the pre-Qin Period, the concept of etiquette and music education was formed. There are books on etiquette, such as *The Book of Rites*, *Rites*, and *Rites of Zhou*. "Being cultured and reasonable" is the pursuit of life in Chinese traditional society. In the Central Plains, the culture of rites and music has a long history. The Zhou government administered Luoyi (today's Luoyang) and made rites and music. In the Central Plains, the rites and music culture gradually sank from the upper nobility to the folk, and combined with the life etiquette in daily life, forming a situation of interaction between etiquette and customs. The Central Plains emphasizes "reciprocity". and pays special attention to important life etiquette. Childbirth, marriage, and funeral are important events in life. They are not only related to the growth of individuals, but also related to the rise and fall of families and the succession of families. Therefore, there are a variety of rituals and customs. According to different purposes and colors of life rituals held in the Central Plains, they are divided into "red events" and "white events". Red events mainly refer to some festive and lively rituals, including weddings, birth ceremony, and birthday ceremony, etc., which advocate red festive colors. White events mainly refer to funerals, with solemn and holy white as the main color of the ceremony.

I. Birth Ceremony

Having children has been highly valued in the Central Plains since ancient times. Young couples who have just got married often receive congratulatory messages "Happy marriage, early childbirth". It is the wish of all the mothers of grooms to have big fat grandsons. The folk in Henan Province have formed a set of customs from seeking children, pregnancy to the birth and upbringing of babies, showing respect for life.

1. Praying for Bearing Children

In the primitive society, people did not realize that procreation was the result of the combination of two sexes and regarded pregnancy as the connection between man and God or a divine gift. There are many myths about pregnancy among the people, such as Hou Ji, the ancestor of the Zhou Dynasty, who was

娘娘、送子观音、王母娘娘等，女性神居多，也有祭拜人祖伏羲等求子的。在求子时一般要烧香、敬奉供品、许愿和还愿，人们认为向神灵求子实现后一定要按照之前的承诺来还愿，否则会受到惩罚。此外，在中原还有"摸子孙窑""拴娃娃"和"摸秋"等有趣求子习俗。随着社会发展，民间求子习俗也在发生着一定变化。现在婚后不孕的青年夫妻更多是到医院检查治疗。

鹿邑太清宫求子的娃娃殿（霍志刚摄）
The Baby Hall of Seeking Children in Taiqing Palace in Luyi
(Photographed by Huo Zhigang)

2. 怀孕

中原民间称婚后女子怀孕为"有喜了"，孕妇多受到家人的各方面照顾，也有很多禁忌以保证母子平安。以往孕妇在饮食方面有禁忌，如不准吃兔肉、鸭肉等。此外，孕妇还忌在夏夜露宿，忌参加红白喜事，忌隔着门槛伸手接递食盐或伸头外望，恐怕因此导致胎位不正或难产。以上禁忌有一些科学合理成分，如孕期饮食注意不乱吃，不频繁参加聚众场合导致疾病感染等。饮食方面除了清淡饮食之外，适当会给孕妇增

born after his mother stepped on a huge footprint, and Qi, the ancestor of the Shang Dynasty, who was born after his mother ate bird eggs, etc. so that in the feudal society, emperors created myths of being born by dragons and stars in order to deify their birth. In the folk, there is a custom of asking gods for children, especially for couples who have been infertile after marriage.

People in the Central Plains worship many gods when they pray for bearing children, such as Songzi Niangniang, Zisun Niangniang, Songzi Guanyin and the Queen Mother, etc. most of whom were goddesses in charge of childbirth, and some worship the ancestor Fuxi and other gods for bearing children. When asking for a child, people usually burn incense, offer offerings, make a wish, and repay a wish. People believe that when their prayers are answered, they must keep their promise and repay their wish, otherwise they will be punished. In addition, there are other interesting child seeking customs in the Central Plains, such as "Touching descendants' kiln", "Tying dolls" and "Moqiu" (a custom for seeking children). The folk customs of seeking children change over time. Now young couples who are infertile are more likely to go to hospital for examination and treatment.

披红送旗杆的孩子（霍志刚摄）
The Child in Red Sending a Flagpole (Photographed by Huo Zhigang)

2. Pregnancy

When a wife is found to be pregnant, people in the Central Plains will say she "has happiness". Pregnant women are often taken special care of by their families, and there are also many taboos to ensure the safety of mothers and babies. In the past, pregnant women were forbidden to eat such food as rabbit

加营养餐等，保证均衡饮食。

3. 分娩和坐月子

孕妇到了预产期并出现分娩征兆时，家人立即做好分娩准备，依照传统习俗要在丈夫家生下孩子，不能回娘家或在别家出生，所以孕妇临产期一般都不外出。过去是请来富有经验的老年妇女，俗称"接生婆"或"喜娘"，孕妇分娩坐在床前放置的矮凳或大盆上，称为"临盆"。产房只许接生者和孕妇的长辈出入，胎儿出生俗称"落地"，胎儿落地后接生者首先用剪刀将"脐带"剪断，敷上艾灰等，然后用事先准备好的衣服将婴儿包好。产妇分娩后在家休养一个月，俗称"坐月子"，在产妇门口挂上红布条，提醒人们注意，也起到"避邪"作用。现在随着医疗水平和生活条件改善，孕妇一般到医院接生，饮食也更加营养均衡。

4. 庆贺

婴儿出生之后，要向亲友报喜，尤其重要的是向婴儿姥姥家报喜，过去生下男孩和女孩的报喜有所不同。三门峡一带生男孩报喜时拿油条、麻糖或鞭炮，生女孩报喜时拿油饼、花朵。沁阳一带则生男孩报喜拿烧饼，生女孩拿麻糖，当地因此将女孩戏称为"麻糖"。豫南商城人生男孩报喜在礼物上放本书，生女孩则放一朵花，寓意男孩多读书成才，女孩长得像花一样。也有地方给婴儿姥姥送公鸡和母鸡来区分男孩和女孩。

婴儿出生三天，要举行"洗三"仪式，用艾草煮水给婴儿沐浴，认为可以使得婴儿健康成长。沐浴时，浴盆中多放硬币10枚，取"十全十美"之意。婴儿的奶奶在沐浴中要用一个

长命锁
A Longevity Lock

meat and duck meat. In addition, pregnant women should also avoid sleeping out on summer nights, participating in weddings and funerals, reaching for salt, or looking out across the threshold, which might lead to incorrect fetal position or dystocia. There are some scientific and reasonable ingredients in these taboos, such as not eating disorderly during pregnancy, or not frequently participating in gatherings, which might lead to disease infection. In terms of diet, in addition to light diet, appropriate nutrition meals will be made to pregnant women to ensure a balanced diet.

3. Childbirth and Confinement

When the date of delivery was due and there were signs of delivery, the family of pregnant woman should immediately prepare for delivery. According to traditional customs, she should give birth at her husband's house and could not go back to her mother's or other people's house. Therefore, pregnant women usually do not go out during the perinatal period. In the past, experienced elderly women were invited, commonly known as "Midwives" or "Xi Niang". A pregnant woman sat on a low stool or large basin placed in front of the bed during childbirth, which was called "labor". Only the midwife and the elders of the pregnant woman were allowed in the delivery room. The birth of the baby was commonly known as "landing". After the baby was born, the midwife first cut off the "umbilical cord" with scissors, applied wormwood ash, etc. and then wrapped the baby with the clothes prepared in advance. After the childbirth, the lying-in woman rested at home for one month, commonly known as "confinement", and a red cloth strip was hung on the door of the pregnant women to remind people to pay attention and to ward off evil spirits. Today, with the improvement of medical treatment and living conditions, pregnant women usually go to hospital for delivery, and their diet is more nutritious and balanced.

4. Celebration

After a baby is born, it is necessary to report the good news to relatives and friends, especially to the mother's family. In the past, the ways of delivering the news of giving birth to boys or girls were different. In the Sanmenxia area, when a boy was born, fried dough sticks, sesame candy or firecrackers were taken to the mother's family, and when a girl was born, oil cakes and flowers were taken. In the Qinyang area,

煮熟的鸡蛋从婴儿头顶开始,向下身滚动,直滚至脚底,一边滚还要一边祈祷着"滚滚头,一辈子不用愁;滚滚手,富贵年年有;滚滚脚,长大能登科"等,然后给婴儿穿上准备好的衣服。

孩子满月或一百天,要为庆祝孩子诞生大摆宴席,请村里人和亲戚朋友都过来热闹。亲友也会送上鸡蛋、面粉、棉被、棉袄、红包等表示祝贺。满月婴儿要理发,俗称"剃胎毛",现在还会给孩子照满月的相册以示纪念。婴儿满月姥姥来做满月时,依照传统会将"长命锁"挂在外孙脖子上,希望孩子能够长命百岁,活泼壮实。

孩子长到一岁成为"一生儿",要举行"抓周"活动。家人向神灵和祖先祷告烧香,然后煮鸡蛋和面条让孩子吃下,之后开始抓周来占卜孩子的前程。家长将一些职业相关的器物摆放在孩子四周,让孩子自己去抓,来看孩子以后从事什么职业。比如抓到书认为孩子以后从事教师等文职工作,抓到枪则预示孩子将来会当兵,抓到秤杆预示孩子以后会成为商人。在民间对于抓周的结果并不是十分在意,更多的是一种娱乐活动,也寄托了家长们对孩子成人成才的期望。

抓周
Drawing Lots

sesame cakes were taken to report the news of the birth of boys, while sesame candy was taken to deliver the news of the birth of girls. Therefore, girls were jokingly called "sesame candy" in the local area. In Shangcheng, south of Henan province, when a boy was born, people put a book on the gift of delivering news, and when a girl was born, a flower was put on the gift with the wish that boys would become talents through more studies and girls would look like flowers. Cocks and hens were taken to deliver the news of the birth of boys and girls in some other places.

Three days after the baby is born, a washing ceremony should be held to bathe the baby with boiled wormwood water, which is believed to make the baby grow healthily. In his or her bath, ten coins are put into the bathtub, which means "perfection". The baby's grandmother should use a boiled egg to roll from the top of the baby's head to the bottom of the baby's feet in the bath. While rolling, she prays that "rolling the egg on the head drives away all worries; rolling the egg on the hands brings wealth every year; rolling the egg on the feet brings honour and rank", and then dresses the baby on prepared clothes.

When a baby is one month or a hundred days old, a large banquet should be held to celebrate the birth of child, and the villagers, relatives and friends should be invited to come and have fun. Relatives and friends will also send eggs, flour, quilts, cotton padded jackets and red envelopes to congratulate. A one-month-old baby needs a haircut, which is commonly known as "shaving fetal hair". Photos will be taken to commemorate. When the baby's grandmother comes to the banquet, she will hang the "Longevity lock" on the grandson's neck according to tradition, hoping that the child can live a long life, lively and strong.

When a baby reaches the age of one, a "Drawing lots" ceremony will be held. The family pray to gods and ancestors, burn incense, boil eggs and noodles for the baby to eat, and then begin to choose an object which symbolizes his or her future. Parents put some career related objects around the baby and let him or her choose to see what their child will do in the future. For example, if he chooses a book, they think that their child will be engaged in civilian work such as teaching. If he chooses a gun, it indicates that their child will become a soldier in the future. If he chooses a scale, it means that their child will become a businessman in the future. People don't care much about the results. It's more an entertainment activity, and it also meets parents' expectations.

二、婚礼习俗

婚姻是人生中之大事，关乎个人和家庭幸福，所以中原地区对婚礼十分重视，也尤为隆重。婚姻习俗相传始于伏羲女娲，而至少到周代时期，已经形成完善的婚姻制度，有所谓的"六礼"：纳采、问名、纳吉、纳征、请期、亲迎。中原地区民间传承的婚礼是在"六礼"基础上发展变化出来的，大致包括择偶、订婚、结婚等阶段。中原地区的婚礼以红色为主要色调，喜庆祥和热闹，注重礼仪，延续着许多古老习俗，充满象征色彩。新婚宴尔、家庭和睦、传宗接代是婚礼习俗的主要追求。

1. 择偶

河南民间将男子择偶称为"找媳妇儿""找对象"，大多数都在子女成年之际开始张罗择偶。在择偶前向往婚姻的青年男女会有各种求姻缘的习俗，如向月老祈求美好姻缘，向伏羲女娲求良伴，七夕向牛郎织女求姻缘等。民间择偶一般讲究"门当户对"，择偶的标准有外貌、身高、家庭条件、工作收入、有无房车等。

民间择偶第一步是提亲，即"六礼"中的"纳采"，俗称"说媒""说亲"。媒人被称为"说媒的""月老"或"红娘"，来往于男女方之间，介绍各自的情况，有双方早已相互了解的也请媒人来穿针引线。过去提亲后要进行"合婚"，也称为"合八字"，即"六礼"之中的"问名"。男女两家将子女姓名和出生的年、月、日、时采用天干地支的八个字写在红纸帖上，互换庚帖，然后请算命先生来算男女双方生辰八字是否相合。如果八字相合，便可以"相亲"，目的是创造机会，让男女双方及其父母能够见上一面，看双方是否中意，若中意则进一步商量婚事。

II. Wedding Customs

Marriage is a major event in life, which is related to personal and family happiness. Therefore, people in the Central Plains attach great importance to weddings, which are especially grand. The marriage custom was handed down from the time of Fuxi and Nüwa. At least until the Zhou Dynasty, a perfect marriage system had been formed, with the so-called "Six Etiquettes" (the six ceremonies of betrothal and marriage): accepting gifts, asking names, accepting auspiciousness, accepting levies, asking for time, and welcoming each other. The folk weddings in the Central Plains develop and change on the basis of the "Six Etiquettes", which roughly include the stages of mate selection, engagement, marriage, etc. The wedding ceremony in the Central Plains is mainly in red. It is festive, auspicious, lively, and values etiquette. It includes many ancient customs and is quite symbolic. Wedding banquets, family harmony and family succession are the main pursuits of wedding customs.

1. Mate Selection

Henan people refer to men's spouse selection as "looking for a wife" or "looking for a partner". Most of them begin to plan for spouse selection when their children reach adults. There are various customs of seeking marriage for young men and women who yearn for marriage, such as praying for a better marriage to Yuelao (the god who unites persons in marriage), Fuxi and Nüwa, and Cowherd and Weaver Girl on the seventh evening of the seventh month. People generally pay attention to "equal marriage" in choosing a spouse. The criteria for choosing a spouse include appearance, height, family conditions, work income, availability of cars and houses, etc.

The first step to choose a spouse is to propose a marriage, that is, "Nacai" (acceptance) in the "Six Etiquettes", commonly known as "matchmaking". Matchmakers are known as "Yuelao" or "Hongniang". They come and go between men and women to introduce their respective situations. If both sides have already known each other, they also invite matchmakers to make the match. In the past, after raising a marriage proposal, "Hehun" was the next step, also known as

现在随着时代和婚姻观念的变化,也有不请媒人就举行婚礼者,属于自由恋爱,民间称为"自谈",更多通过学习、工作、朋友介绍等相互了解。此外,测"生辰八字"的习俗已经减少,更多出于男女双方自愿结合。

2. 订婚

中原地区择偶之后要有订婚仪式,是"六礼"之中"纳吉""纳征"之礼的演变。两家同意联姻之后,先换"允贴",其内容有固定的程式,大意为同意双方联姻,希望能够结秦晋之好。为了使婚姻正式定下来,民间以往还要"传大吉",即"六礼"之"纳征",双方交换上面印有金色龙凤图案的订婚专用红帖,寓意龙凤呈祥,其内容包括联姻的敬语、双方姓名和年庚、媒人姓名等,有证书的作用。这一仪式表示两家婚姻正式确定下来,不可轻易反悔,订婚时间一般选择农历的偶数月和偶数日,意为"好事成双"。订婚时男女双方还要设宴庆贺,有订婚的聘礼,古代聘礼有大雁等,象征坚贞不移的爱情,现在包括金银首饰、现金等。现在订婚前后,还要到地方民政部门领取结婚证,成为合法夫妻,受到法律保护。

聘礼
Betrothal Gifts

"Hebazi," which was "name asking" in the "Six Etiquettes". Both sides exchanged red cards with their names, dates of birth in the eight characters of Heavenly Stems and Earthly Branches on them, and then asked the fortune teller to calculate whether the eight characters of their birthdays matched. If the eight characters matched, "A blind date" could be made. The purpose was to create an opportunity for both the man and woman and their parents to meet and see whether they liked each other. If they liked each other, they could further discuss the marriage.

Today, with changes of times and marriage concepts, there are also people who hold weddings without inviting matchmakers. They fall in love freely, which is called "free love" among the people. They get to know each other through study, work, friends, etc. In addition, the custom of "Hebazi" is not popular and increasingly young people marry for love.

2. Engagement

There should be an engagement ceremony after a mate is chosen in the Central Plains, which is the evolution of "Naji" and "Nazheng" of the "Six Etiquettes". If the two families agree on marriage, they first exchange the "permission sticker", which has a fixed procedure to the effect that they agree to marry and the two families form a marriage alliance. To formalize the marriage, people used to "Spread great good luck", that is, "Nazheng" of the "Six Etiquettes". The two sides exchanged special red posts for engagement printed with golden dragon and phoenix patterns on it, which implied the auspiciousness of the dragon and the phoenix. The contents included the honorific words of the marriage, the names of both parties, dates of their birth, and the names of the matchmaker, which had the function of certificates. This ceremony means that the marriage between the two families has been officially determined and cannot be easily reversed. The engagement time is generally the even months and even days of the lunar calendar, which means "Good things come in pairs". At the time of engagement, both men and women hold a banquet to celebrate. There are betrothal gifts. In ancient times, there were wild geese and so on, which symbolized faithful love. Today, betrothal gifts are gold and silver jewelry, cash and so on. Before and after the engagement, they must go to the local civil affairs department to get a marriage certificate and become legal couples and are protected by law.

3. 婚日礼

中原称结婚为"办喜事""完亲",男方为"娶媳妇儿",女方家为"嫁闺女"或"闺女出门",这是人生中最喜庆热闹的时刻之一。结婚要确定大婚日期,并迎接新娘拜堂成亲,相当于"六礼"中的"请期"和"亲迎"。民间选择结婚日期,俗称"看好儿",会请懂得黄道吉日的人来预卜婚期。婚期选定后,再备礼携带婚书去通知女方,俗称"送好儿"。之后,亲友和街坊邻居向女方家送礼,如布料、衣服、被子、梳妆用品等,这些礼品在结婚日要统一装入箱柜中陪嫁,称为"添箱"。

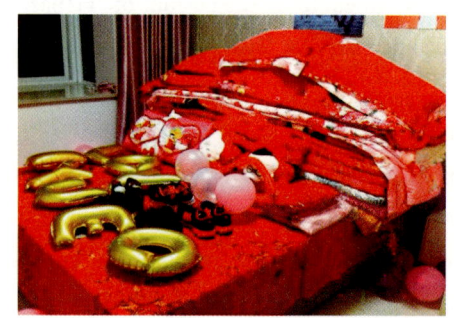

添箱的被子、衣服等
Quilts, Clothes, etc. Sent to the Bride

结婚前一天,男方再次向女方赠送礼物,称"下礼",其中必不可少的是新娘的嫁衣,旧时以红棉袄居多,现在嫁衣有红色和白色婚纱等,还有敬酒穿的旗袍等。结婚前夜,男方家需要布置好新房,张挂红色灯笼、贴红双喜、铺上红色床单被子。新郎此夜宿在新房,还有侄子等孩子陪伴压床,称为"暖房",以此求子。暖房之夜,有地方还要请长辈子孙健全的妇女铺床,唱"铺床歌",把花生、糖果、红枣等抛撒给看热闹的人。

结婚当天,要行迎娶礼。新郎要去女方家迎亲,若女方家较远则前一天安排在较近的亲戚家或宾馆,当天再前往迎娶。民间迎娶的工具随着时代发生变化,在20世纪50年代之前多用花轿迎亲,一路吹吹打打

3. Wedding Ceremony

In the Central Plains, a wedding is called "having a happy occasion". For the bridegroom's side, it is called "marrying a wife", and for the bride's side, it is called "marrying a daughter" or "a daughter going out". This is one of the most festive and lively moments in life. To get married, the date of the grand wedding should be set, and the bride should be welcomed to perform the formal wedding ceremony, which is equivalent to the "Qingqi" (seeking approval by the bride's family of a wedding date selected by the bridegroom's family) and "Qinying" (the bridegroom's going to the bride's room to meet her for the wedding) in the "Six Etiquettes". Folk people choose the date of marriage, commonly known as "Kanhao". People who know the auspicious days will be invited to choose the date of the wedding. After the wedding date is selected, gifts should be prepared and taken to inform the bride's family of marriage date, which is commonly known as "Songhao" (informing the bride's family the date and asking for agreement). Later, relatives, friends and neighbors send gifts to the bride's family, such as cloth, clothes, quilts, toiletries, etc. These gifts should be put into boxes and cabinets for dowry on the wedding day, which is called "Tianxiang".

The day before the wedding, the bridegroom's side again presents gifts to the bride, called "Xiali" (sending gifts), of which the bride's wedding dresses were indispensable. In the old days, most of the dresses were red cotton padded jackets. Now the wedding dresses are usually red and white wedding dresses, as well as the cheongsam for toast. On the eve of the wedding, the bridegroom's family needs to decorate the new house, hang red lanterns, paste double happiness, and make the bed with red sheets and quilts. The bridegroom sleeps in his new house this night, and his nephew and other children accompany him to sleep on the bed, which is called "house warming" to ask for a son. On the night of the house warming in some places, healthy women of the elders with descendants are invited to make the bed, sing the "bed making song", and throw peanuts, candy, red dates and so on to people.

On the wedding day, a wedding ceremony should be held. The groom will go to the bride's house to escort her back to the wedding. If the bride's house is far away, he will stay at a nearby relative's house or a hotel the day before, and then go to the bride's house on the wedding day. The vehicles of folk wedding change

好不热闹;之后结婚用马车、自行车、农用机动车等;现在多用轿车车队来迎亲,领头车子上用鲜花摆成红心,各车镜子上都绑上红绳表示喜车。迎亲队伍出发时,放响鞭炮,响器班奏乐,新郎披红挂花,由亲友陪伴去接新娘,花轿或车内坐着一个侄子辈儿儿童,叫作"压轿孩"。女方家在门口迎接男方,新郎向女方父母叩拜,表示今后要照顾好新娘,孝敬二老。依照传统习俗,新娘要盖上红盖头,怀揣镜子,手抱花瓶,寓意"平平安安",由兄弟或女客搀扶上轿。而现在男方到女方家娶亲,新娘的闺蜜们还会在门口拦着新郎,并将新娘的鞋子藏起来,设置重重障碍来考验新郎,最后冲破障碍的新郎终于抱上新娘上轿车返回。以往

迎亲
Escorting the Bride to the Wedding

over time. Before the 1950s, bridal sedans were used to escort the bride, and the whole journey was lively with drum beating and trumpet blowing; later, carriages, bicycles, agricultural vehicles, etc. were used. Today, a fleet of automobiles are used. The leading cars are decorated with red hearts with flowers, and red strings are tied to the mirrors of each car to show their joy. When the wedding procession departs, firecrackers are fired, trumpets are blown, and the bridegroom wears red flowers, and relatives and friends accompany him to welcome the bride. In the bridal sedan chair or car sits the bridegroom's nephew, called an "accompanying child". People on the bride's side greet the bridegroom at the gate and the bridegroom kowtows to the bride's parents, saying that he would take good care of her and honor the two elders in future. According to the traditional custom, the bride should cover her head with a red cap, carry a mirror, and hold a vase in her hand, which means "Peace and security", and be supported to the sedan chair by her brother or female guests. Now that the bridegroom goes to the bride's house, the bride's friends will stop the groom at the door, hide the bride's shoes, and set up many obstacles to test the groom. The groom who breaks through the obstacles finally takes the bride to the sedan chair. In the past, there was a custom of crying at the wedding ceremony when the bride got married, which indicated that she was reluctant to give up her parents. Now she can go back to her mother's home at any time and crying at the wedding ceremony is rare.

When the wedding procession returns to the front of the groom's house, the bride can't touch the ground when she gets off the sedan chair. In the old days, she walked along the red carpet or reed mat paved on the ground. Sometimes she even stepped on a cloth bag, which meant "carrying on the family line". In some places, a bride might walk over a fire basin, which meant "life will be booming"in the future and could also drive away evil spirits. The heaven and earth table is placed in the main hall of the groom's house, and a ceremony will be held to the sound of music, also known as "heaven and earth worship". The bride and the groom stand in front of the table of heaven and earth, their parents sit in front of them, and the ceremony host shouts, "Firstly, bow to heaven and earth; secondly, bow to your parents; finally, bow to each other". After the wedding ceremony, the couple become a formal couple, and they also drink cross-cupped wine and eat melons and fruits together. The ceremony host would also throw sweets at

新娘出嫁还有哭嫁习俗,表示对父母的不舍之情,现在随时可以回娘家,哭嫁已经很少。

当迎亲队伍返回到新郎家门前时,新娘下轿子不能沾地,旧时沿着地上铺好的红毯或苇席前行,有时还要踩着布袋,寓意"传宗接代";还有跨过火盆,寓意今后的日子"红红火火",也可驱邪。在新郎家正堂中摆放天地桌,新人在乐曲声中举行拜堂仪式,又称"拜天地"。新郎新娘并立于天地桌前,父母端坐在前,执事人高喊"一拜天地,二拜高堂,夫妻对拜"。拜堂成亲后一对新人成为正式夫妻,还要喝交杯酒,一起吃瓜果。执事人还要向前来观看的亲友抛洒糖果,宴会庆祝,好不热闹。新郎新娘换装之后,要向参加婚礼的亲友一一敬酒表示感谢。宾客们要给一对新人送上诚挚的祝福,并赠予红包。

拜堂成亲
Formal Bows by a Bride and a Groom

新郎新娘进入洞房,床上早已用红枣、花生、桂圆、莲子摆成了"新婚快乐"四个大字。新郎的妹妹或嫂嫂要给新房送灯,口里念祝福词。

洞房

Celebrating Wedding in Bridal Chamber

the relatives and friends. The banquet is lively. After the groom and bride change their clothes, they should toast to the relatives and friends attending the wedding. Guests should send sincere wishes and red envelopes to the couple.

When the bride and groom enter the bridal chamber, on their bed, red dates, peanuts, longans, and lotus seeds have long been placed on the bed as four Chinese characters "新婚快乐" (Happy marriage). The groom's sister or

各地还有"入洞房礼",花样繁多。中原各地还有闹洞房的习俗,看热闹的儿童会争相撕扯新房窗户上的红纸,甚至还有各种恶作剧来戏弄新人,俗称"三天之内无大小""越闹越发"。

婚床
A Wedding Bed

婚后第三天,新娘要和新郎第一次回娘家,俗称"回门"。有些地方当天会有新娘的哥嫂带着饺子等礼来接新娘和新郎,有些地方则是新娘偕新郎直接回娘家。新郎到岳父家要行祭祖礼并拜见长辈,然后女家设宴招待。回门者须在日落以前返回婆家。此后节日期间,新郎须陪新娘回娘家,孝敬长辈,传报喜讯。

sister-in-law should send a lamp to the bridal chamber and say blessings. There are also various activities for the entering of the bridal chamber. There is also the custom of spree in the bridal chamber in all parts of the Central Plains. The children watching the fun will scramble to tear the red paper on the window of the bridal chamber, and even play all kinds of pranks to tease the new couple. It is commonly known as "no distinction between old and young in three days" and "the more lively, the more flouring the life will be".

On the third day after the wedding, the bride and the groom will go back to the bride's parental house for the first time, commonly known as "Huimen". In some places, the bride's brother and sister-in-law will come with dumplings and other gifts on that day and take the bride and the groom back. In some places, the bride and the groom will go directly to her parental house. When the bridegroom comes to his father-in-law's house, he must pay tribute to the bride's ancestors and meet her elders, and then the bride's family will hold a banquet. The bride and the groom must return to the groom's house before sunset. After that, on festivals, the groom must accompany the bride back to her parental house, honor her elders and send good news.

三、祝寿礼俗

中原地区注重孝道文化,以四世或五世同堂为理想家庭模式,孝敬老人成为人们所奉行的家庭美德。河南民间盛行为老人祝寿的礼俗,一般60岁之后可以为老人做寿,老人进入寿年,子孙、亲友便要举行一年一度的生日庆祝活动,逢十或吉祥数字岁数更为重视,尤其以60、66、80、100岁的寿诞仪式最为隆重。一旦为老人祝寿,以后年年不能中断,每逢生日儿女甥婿都要前来庆祝。

为老人祝寿当天,要宴请宾客。儿女要将祝寿的厅堂布置停当,悬挂寿星图。亲朋好友所送的寿联、寿幛悬挂两边,常见的寿联有"福如

寿星图
Shouxing (The God of Longevity)

III. Birthday Celebration and Customs

People in the Central Plains attach great importance to the culture of filial piety, taking the four or five generations living together as the ideal family model. Filial piety to the elderly has become a family virtue pursued by people. The folk custom of celebrating the birthday of the elderly is popular in Henan. Generally, people can celebrate the birthday of the elderly after the age of 60. When the elderly enters the birthday year, their descendants, relatives and friends will hold an annual birthday celebration. The number of years on ten or auspicious years is more important, especially the birthday ceremony of 60, 66, 80 and 100 years old. Once the old people's birthday is celebrated, it cannot be interrupted. Every birthday, his children and nephews will come to celebrate.

On the birthday of the old people, a banquet should be held. The children should properly arrange the hall for birthday celebration and hang the Shouxing (the god of longevity) map. The longevity couplets and Shouzhang (a large, oblong sheet of silk with an appropriate message attached, presented at birthday) sent by relatives and friends are hung on both sides. Common longevity couplets include "As beatific as the water which is forever flowing in Donghai Sea, as longevous as the pinasters which are never old in Nanshan Mountain" etc., and auspicious patterns such as "Wuzi Dengke" and "Happiness, wealth and longevity". All kinds of birthday foods, such as longevity peach and longevity noodles, are placed on the hall table. People believe that longevity peaches come from the flat peaches of the heavenly queen mother. Eating them can lead to longevity. Longevity noodles are a bowl of noodles cooked with a long piece of noodles and eggs. The old birthday man should eat this piece of longevity noodles without breaking it in the middle. Children and grandchildren who come to celebrate can share the boiled eggs to enjoy the blessings of the old. The old man leads his children to kneel, worship their ancestors, and pray for peace and blessings, and then sits upright. The children kneel to the birthday star one after another according to their seniority, and offer prepared birthday gifts. Then the family sit around the round table, and the old birthday star blows out the candles of the birthday cake, divides the cake and enjoy the birthday banquet.

东海长流水,寿比南山不老松"等,和"五子登科""福禄寿"等吉祥图案。各种祝寿的食品,如寿桃、长寿面摆放于堂桌之上。人们认为寿桃来自天上王母娘娘的蟠桃,吃了可以长寿。而长寿面则是用一根长面条煮成的一碗面,再加入鸡蛋,寿星老要将这根长寿面吃了,中间不能断。而前来祝贺的子孙可以分食煮好的鸡蛋,来沾沾寿星老的福气。寿星老先率儿女等跪拜祖宗,祈安求福,然后端坐正位。子女等依照辈分大小开始纷纷对老人行跪拜礼,还要奉上准备好的祝寿礼品等。然后一家人围坐在圆桌前,让老寿星吹灭生日蛋糕的蜡烛,然后分蛋糕、吃寿宴。

  为老人祝寿除了大摆宴席,张灯结彩,更为热闹的是请大戏,唱几天豫剧来让老人高兴,所点剧目多为脍炙人口和热闹喜庆的内容。整个祝寿仪式寄托了人们健康长寿的美好愿望,也是中原地区孝道文化的诠释。

To celebrate the old people's birthday, there are not only banquets, lanterns, and decorations, but also full-scale operas. Henan opera will be performed for a few days to make the old man happy. Most of the operas are popular and lively. The whole birthday ceremony embodies people's good wishes for health and longevity, and it is also an interpretation of the filial piety culture in the Central Plains.

四、丧葬礼仪

中原地区自古以来都十分重视丧葬，形成了严密烦琐的丧葬礼仪，体现出中原人世代延续的慎终追远、崇宗敬祖的观念。从远古时期中原出土大量的陶器、玉器陪葬品，到商代妇好墓中的珍贵青铜礼器，再到南阳墓葬汉画像和四神云气壁画等，都可以看出中原地区对于丧葬文化的重视。而河洛的邙山一带成为古代贵族墓葬最为集中的地区之一，将此地视为安葬的风水宝地，有"生在苏杭，葬在北邙"的说法。中原地区传统以土葬为主要类型，讲究"入土为安"。

21世纪以来，为节约耕地、防疫卫生等，大力推行火葬，人去世火化之后，仍依照传统放入棺椁后入土下葬，农村和城市都经历了由土葬到火葬的殡仪改革，倡导丧事简办、文明扫墓、以人为本。

中原地区的丧葬习俗礼仪繁多，庄重肃穆，承载着厚重的信仰。一般成年人丧葬仪式要持续五到七天，十分隆重，之后还有相应的祭奠仪式，以白色为主要基调，又称"白事"，既有对逝者的悼念之情，也寄托了生者对美好生活的向往。

1. 寿终得际

老人在弥留之际，儿女要侍奉守候在身边，听取老人的遗嘱和遗愿，为老人送终，这是对父母养育之恩的报答。为了确定逝者是否安息，要将新绵置于口鼻前，视其是否有气，或者俯身倾听老人的心跳是否停止。当确认老人去世，守候的儿女开始号啕大哭，表达自己的哀痛之情。老人去世不能说"死了"，要称"老了"或"走了"。

IV. Funeral Etiquette

Since ancient times, people in the Central Plains have attached great importance to funerals and a strict and cumbersome funeral etiquette has been formed, which reflects the concept of being cautious in the end and pursuing the future, and worshiping ancestors that people in the Central Plains have cherished for generations. From many pottery and jade funerary objects of ancient times unearthed in the Central Plains, to the precious bronze ritual vessels in the tomb of Fuhao of Shang Dynasty, to the Han portraits and the murals of "Sishenyunqi" in Nanyang Tomb, we can see that the Central Plains attaches importance to funeral culture. The Mang Mountain area in Heluo was one of the most concentrated areas of ancient noble tombs. It was regarded as a geomantic treasure land for burial. There is a saying "Born in Suzhou and Hangzhou, buried in North Mang Mountain". In the Central Plains, the main type of traditional burial is earth burial, which stresses "Peace in the earth".

Since the 21st century, cremation has been vigorously promoted for the sake of arable land and epidemic prevention and sanitation. After people die and are cremated, their ashes are still buried in the earth after being placed in coffins according to the tradition. Both rural and urban areas have experienced the funeral reform from earth burial to cremation, which advocates simple funerals, civilized tomb sweeping and is people-oriented.

There are many funeral customs and rituals in the Central Plains, which are solemn and respectful, carrying a heavy faith. Generally, the funeral ceremony for adults lasts five to seven days, which is very grand. Then there is a corresponding memorial ceremony, with white as the main tone, also known as "Baishi" (white events), which not only mourns the dead, but also reposes the living's yearning for a better life.

1. The End of One's Life

When an old person is dying, his children should attend upon and wait beside him (her), listen to his (her) will and wishes, and carry out the funeral duties. This is a reward for the upbringing of the parents. In order to determine whether

2. 小敛

当老人气已断，体未僵硬时，要为其洗身整容，称为"净身"，象征性地抹澡，以便其"上路"时顺当无碍。一般习惯父走子为其净身，母走女为其净身。净身时讲究"前七后八"，在逝者身前擦洗七下，身后擦洗八下。子女要为逝者换上寿衣，嘴里含饭，或含珠、含铜钱。有些地方的规矩是不能让亡人躺在原先的床上，要放在木板或草铺搭成的灵床上。灵床前下方还有为亡人照路的"长明灯"，旁边还放着一底部钻有小孔的瓦盆，孝子每顿饭都向里面添饭，俗称"老盆"，下葬时由孝子负责摔老盆。亡人之身安排好后，孝子们放声大哭，称为"举哀"。

3. 报丧

家中有人亡故，要派人告知亲友，参加安葬事宜，称为报丧。安葬日期由懂阴阳的人测算出来，一般采用逝后单数日，多排五或排七埋。报丧多由孝子亲往，尤其是母亲丧葬多受娘家的影响，需要特别慎重，尤其尊重舅舅的意见。孝子报丧时穿戴白色孝衣，有诸多规矩，一般只能在门外报丧，不能进入别人家门，以免带去不吉利。

4. 大殓

大殓俗称"入棺"，将亡者尸体装入棺木，是告别遗体的重要礼俗。棺材选定十分讲究，过去以桐木或榆木居多，现在多用订制的石棺。孝子将亡者寿衣整齐，全体止哀，由子女一起将遗体抬入棺内。入殓过程中，男女孝子口中不断嘱告亡人放心过去。盖棺时众孝眷不准哭泣，怕逝者留恋不愿离去。等到棺材封口后，方可放声大哭。入殓后的棺木被称为"灵柩"，要抬放在两条长凳上，俗称"升棺"。棺前垂一白幔，前放供桌，摆上水果、肉类、饭菜等供品，置香炉、白烛、灵牌。现在多将亡人的放大相框摆放于灵前正中位置，供孝子贤孙瞻仰、跪拜。

the old person rests in peace, his children would place new cotton in front of the mouth and nose to see if he is breathing, or bend over to listen to whether the old person's heart has stopped. When the old person is confirmed dead, the waiting children begin to wail and express their grief. When an old person dies, "dead" should not be used, but the euphemisms "old" or "gone" are used instead.

2. Dressing up the Dead for the Funeral Service

When the old person breathes his last and his body is not stiff, his body should be washed and his appearance should be tidied up, which is a symbolic bath and called "body cleaning", so that he can leave smoothly. It is a common practice for the son to do it for his father and the daughter for her mother. In the cleaning of the body, "seven times in the front and eight times in the back" should be followed, which means scrubbing seven times in the front of the body and eight times on the back. The son and daughter should dress the deceased with a shroud. Rice, beads, or copper coins should be put into the deceased's mouth. In some places, it is the rule that the deceased should not be allowed to lie in their original beds but should be placed on a wooden or grass bed. In front of and below the mourning bed, there is an "Ever burning lamp" to illuminate the way for the dead. Next to it, there is an earthen basin with a small hole drilled at the bottom. The dutiful son puts food into it for each meal, commonly known as the "Laopen" (old basin). The dutiful son is supposed to throw the old basin at the time of burial. After the body of the deceased is arranged, the filial sons cry loudly, which is called "Juai"(wailing).

3. Giving an Obituary Notice

If someone in the family dies, a person should be sent to inform relatives and friends to attend the funeral, which is called giving an obituary notice. The burial date is calculated by people who know Yin and Yang. Generally, it is an odd number of days after death, and usually the fifth or seventh day. An obituary notice is mostly given by the dutiful sons. The funerals of mothers are often influenced by the families of mothers' side, so they need to be very careful, especially respecting the opinions of uncles. The dutiful sons wear white clothes when announcing the death. There are many rules. Generally, they can only

入殓
Encoffining Ceremony

5. 出殡与安葬

出殡是丧事活动的高潮，择定时间、地点后，做好准备，将棺木下葬，"入土为安"。出殡前为方便亲友吊孝，在院内或大门口搭起灵棚，响器班奏乐。灵棚内还有纸和高粱秆扎成的花圈、房子、电视机、轿车、摇钱树等。出殡早晨，孝子要到祖先堂前祭拜，行辞祖礼。起灵出殡的具体时间上午和下午都有，起灵时鞭炮声响，哀乐大奏，长子抱"灵牌"，长孙扛引魂幡在前面引路，孝子们手拿白色哀杖跟随。抬棺人喊一声"起轿"，然后开始步调一致抬棺前行，遇到前面有坑的道路，前面抬棺者会高喊一声"小心脚步"，后面齐声回应。每到一个大路口，要停灵，孝子们面向灵柩跪地烧纸祭奠，民间称为"路祭"，这时女眷哭声一片，旁边有人负责搀扶。

到达墓地之后，有之前已经挖好的长方形墓室，将棺木安放其中。墓室的选择十分讲究，注重风水，墓室的位置、朝向、深度、大小等都有规定，有民间专门的人员负责。在下葬前，孝子先下墓室烧纸和清理墓室，将土工故意留下的未干的活干完，称最后伺候老人，也称为"抢元宝"。封土时，先从长子开始封土，然后依次相继，将墓室封土至地

announce the death outside the door and cannot enter other people's houses to avoid bringing bad luck.

4. Encoffining Ceremony

The encoffining ceremony is commonly known as "Putting the body into the coffin" and is an important ritual to bid farewell to the body. Coffin selection is very particular. In the past, most coffins were made of paulownia or elm, but now custom-made sarcophagus are used. The dutiful son tidies up the deceased's shroud, all the people stop mourning, sons and daughters carry the body into the coffin together. In the process of encoffining, dutiful sons and daughters tell the deceased to rest assured. When the coffin is closed, all the relatives are not supposed to cry, for fear that the deceased will not leave. After the coffin is sealed, people can cry loudly. The coffin with a body in is called "Lingjiu", which should be lifted and placed on two benches, commonly known as "Coffin lifting". There is a white curtain hanging in front of the coffin, and a supply table is placed in front with fruits, meat, meals and other offerings, and incense burners, white candles, and a spirit tablet on top. Today, the enlarged picture frame of the deceased is placed in the middle of the front of tablet for the dutiful sons and grandchildren to worship.

5. Carrying a Coffin to the Cemetery and Interment

Carrying a coffin to the cemetery is the climax of a funeral. After the time and place are set, and preparations are made, the coffin will be buried. Before the coffin is carried to the cemetery, a mourning shed is set up in the courtyard or at the gate of the house for relatives and friends to mourn, and the trumpet class is invited to play music. There are also wreaths, houses, televisions, cars, money trees and so on made of paper and sorghum stalks. In the morning of the funeral, the dutiful sons should go to the ancestral hall to worship and perform the ceremony of farewell to the ancestors. The specific time for carrying a coffin to the cemetery is in the morning or afternoon. Firecrackers are fired, mourning music is played, and the eldest son holds "The tablet of the spirit", the eldest grandson carries the flag of the soul way, and the dutiful sons follow with white mourning sticks. The coffin lifters shout "Lifting the coffin", and then begin to lift the coffin

平面，然后踏实。在坟前栽一棵柳树或松柏，将纸扎器物和祭品在坟前付之一炬，众孝子磕头祭拜。

扎纸花
Binding Paper

安葬之后，第二天孝子要挨家挨户向亲友酬谢和回送礼，称为"谢孝"。逢七的日子要到坟前烧纸祭奠，尤以"五七"最为重要，除了祭奠亡者，还要摆宴招待亲朋。尊亲去世后一定时期内，孝子要穿孝并停止娱乐，穿白色布鞋，一般守孝期限是三年，三年之内家里过年不能贴门神和对联。每逢春节、清明节、中元节等，还要为逝者扫墓祭拜，以寄托哀思。

送葬队伍
Funeral Procession

in steps. When encountering a road with pits in front, the coffin lifters in front would shout "Watch your step" and the back would respond in unison. At every major intersection, the procession must stop. The dutiful sons kneel to the coffin and burn paper for a memorial, which is called "Road sacrifice". At this time, the female family members will cry, and people nearby are supposed to support them.

The coffin will be placed in a rectangular tomb chamber that has been dug before. The choice of the tomb chamber is very particular. It pays attention to Feng Shui. The location, orientation, depth, and size of the tomb chamber are all regulated, and special folk personnel are in charge. Before burial, the dutiful sons go to the tomb chamber to burn paper and clean it, and finish the unfinished work left by the earthwork, serving the old person for the last time, which is called "Qiang Yuanbao". The heaping earth over mound starts with the eldest son, and the other sons heap the tomb to the ground level in turn, and then they stamp on the earth to make it firm. A willow or pine cypress will be planted in front of the grave, the paper bound objects and sacrifices will be burnt, and the dutiful sons will kowtow and worship.

The day after the burial, the dutiful sons would go door to door to send gifts to express appreciation to relatives and friends for their presence at funerals, which is called "Xiexiao". On every seventh day, they would burn paper in front of the grave to offer a sacrifice, of which "The fifth" is the most important. In addition to offering sacrifices to the deceased, a banquet will be held to entertain relatives and friends. Within a certain period after the death of parents, dutiful sons and daughters should wear mourning and stop entertainment activities. They should wear white cloth shoes. Generally, the period of filial piety is three years. Within three years, the family can't paste door gods and couplets during the Spring Festival. During the Spring Festival, Tomb Sweeping Day and the Zhongyuan Festival, they also sweep the tombs of the deceased and offer sacrifices to express their grief.

第四章

建筑民俗

Chapter 4

Architectural Folklore

中原地区是中华民族的重要发祥地，我国考古发现的著名的原始村落遗址新郑裴李岗文化遗址、渑池仰韶、郑州黄河畔大河村等都在河南境内。其中距今7000～8000年的裴李岗文化发现了石磨盘、石磨棒和锯齿石镰刀等，代表了原始农业和畜牧业发展到相当水平，开始形成了原始定居村落。根据考古发现，这一时期，中原先民已经开始走出自然的洞穴，开始营造人工房舍，起初房舍为半地穴式，在地下挖一坑穴，沿四周接上低墙，中间立以木柱，依木柱搭起屋顶，盖上茅草，这种房子就地取材，是原始穴居和筑巢而居的融合演变。至仰韶文化时期，居住面逐渐上升到地面，房舍空间四壁用"木骨泥墙"构筑，出现了直立的墙体和倾斜的屋盖，有了分成几室的大房子，奠定了后世栋宇住房的基本形式。

中原地区的建筑从居住形式上大体可以分为两大类：一类为地面上修建而起的栋宇式住房，以砖木结构为主，有平房和楼房之分，其区域主要分布于广大平原地区；另一类则是在豫西山地较为常见的传统穴居窑洞，在山崖或地面上挖凿洞穴而形成的居住建筑。

当然，从聚居形态上划分，中原聚居类型又可以分为非农业生产为主要职能、人口相对稠密的城市，以及农业生产为主、人口相对较少的村落。而镇则是介于两者之间，是比村更高一级的行政单位，既有商贸为主的镇，也有兼顾农业生产的镇，中原地区的镇都有定期的集市。中原地区是历代王朝建都最为集中的地区，中国八大古都有四个位于河南，这反映出中国古代"择中而居"的观念。

一、栋宇住房

中原民间栋宇住房形态经历了漫长的发展演变，在20世纪的农村，草房、瓦房、平房、楼房等都可以看到，有明显的年代分期。近年来，农村面貌发生了巨变，居住房屋也开始采用新建筑材料，楼房增多，更

Chapter 4　Architectural Folklore

The Central Plains region is an important birthplace of the Chinese nation. The famous primitive village sites discovered by archaeologists in China, such as the Peiligang Cultural Site, Mianchi Yangshao, Zhengzhou Dahe Village along the Yellow River, are all in Henan. Stone grinding plates, stone roller, and serrated sickles found in the site of Peiligang Culture date back to 7000-8000 years, which represent the development of primitive agriculture and animal husbandry to a considerable level and the formation of primitive settlement villages. According to archaeological findings, in this period, the ancestors of the Central Plains had begun to go out of natural caves and build houses. At first, the houses were half underground. A hole was dug underground, and low walls were connected around it. Wooden columns were erected in the middle, and the roof was built on them and covered with thatch. This kind of house was based on local materials, which was the evolution of primitive cave dwelling and nesting. In the period of Yangshao Culture, the residential area gradually rose to the ground, and the four walls of the building were "Wood structure and mud walls". There were upright walls and inclined roofs, and large houses were divided into several rooms, which laid the basic form of pillar houses in later generations.

In terms of residential forms, the buildings in the Central Plains can be roughly divided into two categories: One is the buildings built on the ground, mainly of brick and wood structures, including bungalows and buildings of two or more stories, which are mainly distributed in the vast plains. The other is the traditional cave dwelling, which is common in the mountains of western Henan. It is a residential building formed by digging caves on the cliff or ground.

In terms of settlement patterns, the settlement types in the Central Plains can be divided into cities with relatively dense population whose main function is non-agricultural production, and villages with relatively small population whose main function is agricultural production. The town is somewhere in between, which is an administrative unit of higher level than the village. There are both trade-oriented towns and towns that give consideration to agricultural production. Towns in the Central Plains have regular fairs. The Central Plains is the most concentrated region for the establishment of capitals of ancient dynasties. Four of the eight great ancient capitals were in Henan, which reflects the concept of "Choosing the middle to inhabit" in ancient China.

加注重室内装修，居住条件得到极大改善。

　　草房是新中国成立前和建国初期河南民间的主要住房形式。其屋架由梁、檩、椽组成，构成"人"字形屋顶，顶部用草覆盖。栋梁房架一般用榆木、杨木、松木树干做成，要结实耐用。顶部覆盖的草有稻草、麦草、菱草等，根据农作物生产情况不同就地取材，每隔几年时间都要修缮更换屋草，以免漏雨。而草房的墙多用泥土夯实而成，或用泥制成泥胚垒砌而成。

传统草房
A Traditional Thatched Cottage

　　瓦房在新中国成立之前多为富裕人家居住，新中国成立之后民间瓦房不断增加，砖瓦房也"飞入寻常百姓家"。原来的瓦房多用弧形小瓦，为青灰色，称"青瓦"或"汉瓦"，后出现了大块的红色机制瓦，还有琉璃瓦等。瓦房房架一般采用"重梁起架"的形式，由大梁、二梁立柱和叉手相连以放檩条，上面鱼鳞一样覆盖瓦片，瓦下铺草或箔席之类，覆以"麦茬泥"，以便瓦片更严密结实覆盖在檩条上，可以防止漏雨。瓦房的墙体用烧制而成的青砖或红砖。在瓦房的房脊和房檐，讲究的人

I. Housing

The formation of housing in the Central Plains has experienced a long period of development and evolution. In the rural areas of the 20th century, thatched cottages, tiled houses, bungalows, and buildings could be seen, with obvious chronological stages. In recent years, great changes have taken place in the rural areas. New building materials have been adopted for residential houses. More buildings have been built. More attention has been paid to indoor decoration, and the living conditions have been greatly improved.

Thatched cottages are the main form of folk housing in Henan Province before and in the early days of the founding of the People's Republic of China. The roof truss is composed of beams, purlins (the horizontal member in the roof supported by the upper chord and supporting the rafters—also called the stringer), and rafters to form a "herringbone" roof, and the top is covered with thatch. The beam frame is generally made of elm, poplar and pine trunks, which are strong and durable. The thatch covered on the top includes straw, wheat straw, etc. depending on different crop production conditions. The thatch shall be repaired and replaced every few years to avoid rain leakage. However, the walls of thatched cottages are mostly compacted with soil or built with clay embryo.

Tile-roofed houses were mostly inhabited by wealthy families before the founding of New China. After the founding of New China, the number of private tile-roofed houses continued to increase, and brick tile-roofed houses also "Flew into the homes of ordinary people". The original tile-roofed houses mostly used small arc tiles, which were cyan gray and called "Green tiles" or "Han tiles". Later, large red machine-made tiles and glazed tiles appeared. Tile-roofed house frames are generally in the form of "heavy beam lifting", which are connected by girders, two beam columns and forks to place purlins. The tiles are covered like fish scales on the top, and grass or foil mats are paved under the tiles, covered with "wheat stubble mud", so that the tiles are more tightly and firmly covered on the purlins, which can prevent rain leakage. The walls of tile-roofed houses are made of burned green bricks or red bricks. Exquisite families will decorate the ridge and eaves of tile-roofed houses with flowers, animals and bizarre animals.

家还会缀上花朵、动物、异兽等造型。

传统瓦房
A Traditional Tile-roofed House

平顶房是顶部不起脊的一层房屋，在新中国成立前是安阳、濮阳一带民房的主要形式。其结构和瓦房一样包括梁、檩、椽，只是屋顶不起脊，顶部覆以砖瓦或用石灰、煤渣、沙土拌泥捶平。20世纪70年代以后，平顶房顶部更多采用水泥和钢筋预制板，用水泥和沙抹平，设置上下楼梯，可以在上面晾晒谷物。有些人家还在通道上部盖一小楼，可以不受风雨侵扰。

传统的石板房主要分布在豫北太行山区的林州、辉县等。其外观构造与瓦房相似，不过墙壁用石块垒成，梁檩上覆盖经过加工制作整齐的薄石板。覆盖石板横向成行，纵向接缝。接缝处再用小石板压盖，屋脊平压石块。这种房屋在山区就地取材，坚固耐用，被民众称为"百年不坏房"，至今这些地区还保留不少石板房。

楼房是两层或两层以上的房屋。中原地区早在仰韶文化时期已有四根柱子支起的双层房屋。商周以后宫殿建筑日渐完善，汉代宫殿和富家大户的楼房更为壮丽恢宏，从出土的不少汉代陶楼可以看出当时的楼房

The flat-roofed house is a one-story house with no ridge on the top. Before the founding of New China, it was the main form of folk houses in Anyang and Puyang. Its structure includes beams, purlins and rafters like tile-roofed houses, but the roof is not ridged, and the top is covered with bricks and tiles or hammered flat with lime, cinder and sand. After the 1970s, cement and reinforced precast slabs were more used on the top of flat-roofed houses, which were plastered with cement and sand, and stairs were set up to dry grains on the roof. Some people also build a small building on the upper part of the passage, which can be protected from wind and rain.

The traditional slate houses are mainly distributed in Linzhou and Huixian in Taihang Mountains in the Northern Henan. Its exterior structure is similar to that of the tile-roofed house, but the walls are built of stones, and the beam purlins are covered with neatly processed thin slates. Slates are put in horizontal rows with longitudinal joints. The joints are covered with small stone slabs, and the roof ridge is flat pressed with stones. This kind of house is made of local materials in mountainous areas. It is strong and durable, which is called a "Century old house" by people. So far, many slate houses have been preserved in these areas.

A building is a house with two or more stories. As early as the Yangshao Culture in the Central Plains, there were two-story houses supported by four columns. After the Shang and Zhou dynasties, the palace buildings became more and more perfect. The palaces of the Han Dynasty and the buildings of wealthy families were more magnificent. From the unearthed pottery buildings of the Han Dynasty, it can be seen that the buildings at that time had several floors, including pavilions, terraces and open halls and cornice corridors. Before the founding of New China, only the rich and big families were able to build buildings. After the reform and opening up, with the improvement of people's living standards and the enhancement of economic strength, the number of buildings in urban and rural areas are increasing day by day. Now they can be seen everywhere, and people of the whole village live in well-planned two or three-story buildings.

The layout forms of the traditional folk houses in the Central Plains are usually three-section compound and quadrangle dwellings, which are composed of main rooms, wing rooms (rooms on the east side and west side) and rooms adjacent to streets. Most of them are "high walls and narrow courtyards". Once

有数层，亭台楼阁、飞檐走廊一应俱全。新中国成立前，只有富家大户才有能力建造楼房，而改革开放之后，随着人民生活水平提高，经济实力增强，城市和农村地区的楼房日渐增多，现在已经是随处可见，甚至整个村子都住上了规划齐整的两三层小楼。

传统的中原民间宅院有三合院、四合院等布局形态，由堂屋、厢房（东西屋）、邻街房组成，多为"高墙窄院"，关上大门后成为一个严密的封闭空间，能够增强安全感，这与中原古代多战乱有一定关系。堂屋一般坐北朝南，便于采光，多为家中老人或主人居住。堂屋多为三间，中间供祖宗牌位或神佛等，是神圣之地，家中有结婚、丧事等大事都要在此祷告。而堂屋的左右房间多为家中老人的卧室，光线好，冬天暖和，是中原地区尊老爱老的体现。而厢房则为子女居住，房屋居住的人员安排讲究长幼有序，渗透着儒家的伦理观念。

林州石板房
Slate Houses in Linzhou

Chapter 4 Architectural Folklore

楼房

A Building

the gates are closed, they become a tight closed space, which can enhance the sense of security. This has something to do with many wars in the Central Plains in ancient times. The central house usually faces south, which is convenient for daylighting and is mostly inhabited by the elderly or the owners. Most of the main rooms have three rooms, with ancestral tablets or gods and Buddhas in the middle. The middle room is a sacred place, where people pray for marriage, funeral and other important events. The left and right rooms of the main rooms are mostly the bedrooms of the elderly. The lighting is good and the winter is warm. It is the embodiment of respecting and loving the elderly in the Central Plains. While the wing rooms are for children to live in. The arrangement of people living in the house pays attention to the order of elders and children, which is permeated with Confucian ethical concepts.

二、穴居窑洞

在豫西山地北部荥阳以西至潼关和豫北太行山区，有传统的穴居窑洞居住方式。这一地区地处黄土高原，土质干燥，直立性好，不易坍塌，为窑洞建造创造了天然的便利条件。

这种窑洞充分利用了黄土高原的土质特性，挖凿方便，开凿出来的窑洞冬暖夏凉，干燥防潮，是与自然生态相契合的一种民居形式。中原窑洞依据建造方式不同，有靠崖窑、地窑（地坑院）、锢窑、房洞结合窑等形式。值得一提的是，中国唐代最伟大的诗人之一杜甫就出生于河南巩义笔架山下的一孔窑洞中，因而这一窑洞被命名为"杜甫诞生窑"，杜甫在此度过了他的童年生活，现在已经修葺建立了杜甫故里纪念馆。杜甫诞生的窑洞就是一座典型的靠崖窑。

1. 靠崖窑

靠崖窑在开挖前要在沟畔崖腹开辟一垂直的崖壁，高约10米，俗称"窑脸"，然后根据其宽度确定开挖窑洞孔数和挖凿位置。一般根据传统以三孔为佳，寓意"福、禄、寿"三星。如果"窑脸"宽度不够，只能挖两孔者，多在两孔间挖一小窑，以敬天神和补三星之不足。开挖时先凿一宽可放置一门框，高可在门框上置一窗，深1.67米左右的小拱形"窑间"，然后扩大，开挖高约3米、宽约3米的拱形窑体。这种窑不需要垒建洞前的窑壁，装上门窗便可居住，优点是省时省工、造价低廉，但窑洞内采光条件一般。而靠崖窑还有另一种建造方式是直接在窑脸上开挖高大的拱形窑体，挖好后再于窑体前与窑脸看齐，垒砌"窑间墙"，墙上一侧设门、一侧设窗户，上部与拱形窑顶接近处设通风出烟口。这种建造方式工料增加，优点是光线充足，窑内更显敞亮舒适。

II. Cave Dwelling

In the northern mountainous area of western Henan, from the west of Xingyang to Tongguan and Taihang mountainous area of Northern Henan, there are traditional cave dwelling ways. This area is located in the Loess Plateau. The soil is dry and upright which is not easy to collapse, creating natural convenient conditions for the construction of the caves.

The caves make full use of the soil characteristics of the Loess Plateau. It is easy to dig. The caves are warm in winter and cool in summer. They are dry and moisture-proof. It is a form of folk houses consistent with the natural ecology. According to different construction methods, there are various kinds of cave dwelling, such as cliff cave dwelling, underground cave dwelling (underground pit yard), Gu cave dwelling, cave dwelling with combination of houses and caves, and other forms. It is worth mentioning Dufu, one of the greatest poets of the Tang Dynasty, was born in a cave dwelling at the foot of Bijia Mountain in Gongyi, Henan Province. Therefore, this cave was named "The Birth Cave of Dufu". Dufu spent his childhood here and it has been repaired and the Memorial Hall of Dufu has been established. The cave where Dufu was born is a typical cliff cave dwelling.

杜甫诞生窑
The Birth Cave Dwelling of Dufu

靠崖窑
A Cliff Cave Dwelling

2. 地坑院

地坑院，又称天井院、地窑，是河南三门峡地区独特的一种民居形式，被称为中国北方的"地下四合院"。在三门峡陕州的高台平原地区至今仍有 100 多个地下村落，保留近万座地坑院。地坑院是先在平地上向下挖出一个长宽各 10 余米、深 8 余米的方形平底天井院落，然后在其四壁凿挖出若干个单孔窑洞，一侧筑有斜坡甬道供人们上下出入。这种民居全在地下，进村望去只见树木道路，却不见房屋村舍，当地人形象地称为"进村不见人，见树不见村"。

地坑院从起源来看是古代先民穴居的遗留，是当地居民因地制宜的产物，有不少优点。它就地取材，省工省料，造价低廉，一户人家几个月便可以凿挖出一座地坑院，可以使用 100 多年。这与当今大城市动辄数百万、上千万购买一套住宅相比可谓是物美价廉，是历经千年沉淀的不动产。地坑院还有冬暖夏凉的特点，适宜人类居住。地坑院处于地下，减少了外界噪音的污染，十分幽静，别有洞天。

1. Cliff Cave Dwelling

Before the excavation of a cliff cave dwelling, a vertical cliff with a height of about 10 meters, commonly known as "the face of the cave dwelling", shall be opened at the cliff belly beside the ditch, and then the number of caves to be excavated and the excavation position shall be determined according to its width. According to the tradition, three caves are preferred, implying "three gods of fortune, wealth and longevity". If "the face" is not wide enough and only two caves can be dug, a small cave shall be dug between the two to worship gods and make up for the shortage of three gods. During excavation, a small arched cave room with a width of one door frame and a height of one window on the door frame and a depth of about 1.67m shall be chiseled first, and then expanded to an arched cave body with a height of about 3 meters and a width of about 3 meters. There is no need to build a wall in front of the cave. It is inhabitable with doors and windows. Its advantages are timesaving, labor-saving and low cost, but the lighting conditions in the cave are general. Another construction method of the cliff cave dwelling is to directly excavate a tall arch body in the face, and then align it with the face in front of the cave body. The cave wall is built. A door is set on one side of the wall, a window is set on the other side, and a ventilation outlet is set at the upper part close to the top of the arched cave. This construction method has the advantages of sufficient light, and the inside of the cave is bright and comfortable.

2. The Silo-cave

The silo-cave, also known as the underground cave dwelling and the pit yard, is a unique form of folk house in Sanmenxia, Henan Province. It is known as the "Underground quadrangle courtyard" in northern China. There are still more than one hundred underground villages in the Gaotai plain of Sanmenxia Shanzhou, and nearly 10,000 underground silo-caves are reserved. The silo-cave is a square courtyard with a length of more than 10 meters, a width of more than 8 meters and a depth of more than 8 meters dug down on the flat ground, and then several caves were dug out in its four walls, and a slope corridor is built on one side for people to go up and down. These dwellings are all underground. When you go to the village, you can only see trees and roads, but not houses and cottages. Local people say "when you go to the village, you can't see people, and when you see

第四章 建筑民俗

地坑院
A Silo-cave Building

地坑院在建造过程中包含不少民俗知识和技艺，可谓独居匠心。它遵循传统的风水观念，讲究阴阳的配合与五行的相生相克。地坑窑中的不同窑洞根据其使用功能可以分为住窑、堂窑、厨窑、库窑、杂窑等，多则十几孔，合成四方窑洞，站在院内看苍穹似圆盖，与中国古代"天圆地方"观念相一致。院内不仅是人们居住之所，连鸡、牛、驴等也有单独的窑洞。还有专做粮仓用的窑洞，顶部开有一个小孔，直通屋顶的打谷场，收获晒干粮食后可以直接将谷场粮食灌进窑内的粮仓，简单省力，平时孔口遮蔽。在院落内还打有水井和用于排水的旱井，如果下雨，雨水可以流入旱井中被干燥的黄土吸得干干净净。

地坑院内生活的居民十分注重生活环境的营造。住人的窑洞有意加大门窗，增加洞内的通风透气和光照，视野更加开阔。院中多栽石榴、

trees, you can't see the village".

From the perspective of origin, the silo-cave is the legacy of ancient cave dwellers. It is the product of local residents' adaptation to local conditions and has many advantages. It uses local materials, saves labor and materials, and the cost is low. A silo-cave can be dug out in a few months, which can be used for more than 100 years. Compared with millions or tens of millions that people spend on a house in big cities today, it is real estate of high quality and reasonable price that has been deposited for thousands of years. The silo-cave is warm in winter and cool in summer, which is suitable for human habitation. It is underground, which is noticeably quiet with less pollution of external noise.

The construction of the silo-cave requires quite a lot of folk knowledge and skills, which can be described as unique ingenuity. It follows the traditional geomantic concept and stresses the coordination of Yin and Yang and the mutual generation and restriction of the five elements. The cave dwellings can be divided into residential cave dwellings, hall cave dwellings, kitchen dwellings, warehouse cave dwellings, miscellaneous cave dwellings, etc. according to their functions. Some silo-caves have more than a dozen caves, which form a square cave dwelling. Seen from the courtyard, the sky looks like a round cover, which is consistent with the ancient Chinese concept of "Round sky and square earth". The courtyard is not only a place for people to inhabit, but also has separate caves for chickens, cows and donkeys. There is also a cave specially used for granary. There is a small hole on top, which leads directly to the threshing ground on the roof. After being harvested and dried, the grain from the grain field can be directly poured into the granary in the cave dwelling. It is simple and labor-saving, and the hole is covered in normal times. There are also water wells and dry wells for drainage in the courtyard. If it rains, the rainwater can flow into the dry wells and be absorbed by the dry loess (a fine-grained unstratified accumulation of clay and silt deposited by the wind).

The residents living in the silo-cave attach great importance to the construction of the living environment. Larger doors and windows are designed for residential caves for better ventilation, lighting and a broader view. Pomegranates, persimmons and other fruit trees are planted in the yard, which can not only yield numerous fruits, but also mean "More children and more blessings, and everything goes well". The local women are dexterous, and they cut various

地坑院

A Silo-cave Building

柿子等果木，不仅可以收获累累果实，也寓意"多子多福，事事如意"。当地的女性心灵手巧，还会剪出各式各样的窗花来装点窑洞的门窗和顶棚，仿佛进入到了民俗艺术的世界。地坑院一般是独门独户，自成院落，如果兄弟分家，可以在附近再开凿出一座地坑院，中间打通，成为多个地坑院的组合，曲径通幽，错落有致，宛如地下的宫殿。近年来，当地还组织举办了陕州地坑院灯会，在元宵佳节赏灯游览，别有风韵。豫西地坑院是黄土地上散落的"明珠"，世世代代居住在这里的民众最能感受到大地的脉搏。

地坑院
A Silo-cave Building

window flowers to decorate the doors, windows and ceilings of the cave. Living there you feel as if you have entered the world of folk art. A silo-cave is usually inhabited by a single family with its own courtyard. If brothers are separated and live apart, other silo-caves can be dug nearby, which can be connected in the middle and a multiple silo-cave form. The winding paths lead to seclusion and are scattered like an underground palace. In recent years, the Lantern Festival of Shanzhou Silo-caves has been organized and held in the local area. To visit the silo-caves and watch lanterns at the Lantern Festival is quite special. The silo-caves in the west of Henan Province are "Pearls" scattered on the loess. People living here for generations can feel the pulse of the earth.

三、中原古镇

中原地区平原面积辽阔，在历史上农业一直占据主要地位。不过随着古代社会经济的发展，尤其是明清时期商业进一步繁荣，中原地处中州，为南北枢纽、东西桥梁，出现了不少传统的集镇和水旱码头。商户在此云集，贸易在此流通，形成了一些著名的商业古镇，在作为地方政治中心的基础上也成了经济和文化中心，具有较大范围的辐射力。这些古镇大都具有便利的交通，或为重要陆上通道，或为水陆码头，有定期举行的集市和庙会，便于进行商品流通。古镇内商铺林立，商人众多，为增强联络，也多修建会馆和庙宇，山陕会馆、关帝庙等建筑大量兴起，其中就有晋商的影响。有些古镇甚至具备了城市的规模，也修筑了高大的城墙和城门，有相对固定的贸易场所和功能分区，街道名字也和商品贸易相关，如瓷器街、牛马街、布衣街等。清朝时期，河南地区形成了四大名镇等称谓，显示出中原商业的繁荣。这些古镇也是地方的文化中心，因为庙宇众多，商客云集，多庙会和社火表演，镇内戏台还多有戏剧演出，成为民间艺术的荟萃之地，常影响到周边村镇的文化。近年来，国家注重古镇的保护与开发，河南地区入选国家历史文化名镇的古镇有10个，成为中原靓丽的文化名片，包括朱仙镇、神垕镇、荆紫关镇、赊店镇、古荥镇、竹沟镇、冢头镇、嵖岈山镇、道口镇、白雀园镇等。

1. 朱仙镇

河南朱仙镇是国家第二批公布的历史文化名镇，位于河南省开封市南约20千米（公里）。明清时期，朱仙镇与佛山镇、景德镇、汉口镇并称为我国四大名镇。朱仙镇历史底蕴深厚，历史遗迹丰富，现存国家级文物保护单位3处，省级文物保护单位2处。朱仙镇因为战国时期名士朱亥的食邑和封地而得名，他从一名隐士到帮助信陵君窃符救赵而一鸣惊人。明清时期，朱仙镇是中原地区重要的水陆码头，运粮河自北而

III. Ancient Towns in the Central Plains

The plain area of the Central Plains is vast, and agriculture occupies a major position in history. However, with the development of ancient social economy, especially the further prosperity of commerce in the Ming and Qing Dynasties, many docks for land and water transport service sprung up, as the Central Plains was located in Zhongzhou (the central region of China), which was the hub between north and south, and the bridge between east and west. With merchants gathering and trade flowing here, some famous commercial towns were formed. Being the local political centers, they also became the economic and cultural centers with a large range of radiation. Most of these ancient towns had convenient transportation. They were either important land passages or docks for land and water transportation service. There were regular fairs and temple fairs to facilitate commodity circulation. There were many shops and merchants in the ancient town. In order to enhance communication, more guild halls and temples were built. Shanshan guild hall, Guandi Temple and other buildings sprung up under the influence of Jin merchants. Some ancient towns even had the scale of a city, with tall walls and gates built, relatively fixed trading places and functional divisions. Street names were also related to commodity trade, such as Porcelain Street, Niuma (cattle and horses) Street, Buyi (cloth) Street, etc. In the Qing Dynasty, four famous towns were established as a result of prosperity of commerce in the Central Plains. These ancient towns are also local cultural centers. Because there were many temples, businessmen, visitors, many temple fairs, Shehuo (traditional festivities), and many theatrical performances on the stage in the towns, towns became the gathering places of folk art and often affected the cultures of surrounding villages and towns. In recent years, the state has paid attention to the protection and development of ancient towns. There are 10 ancient towns selected as national famous historical and cultural towns in Henan, which have become beautiful cultural cards in the Central Plains, including Zhuxian Town, Shenhou Town, Jingziguan Town, Shedian Town, Guxing Town, Zhugou Town, Zhongtou Town, Chayashan Town, Daokou Town, Baiqueyuan Town.

南穿城而过，直通江淮地区。两岸码头林立，商贸繁忙，每日来往船只200余艘，人口有数十万之多。当时镇内寺庙建筑有110多座，仅戏楼就有11座，以明皇宫戏楼为最。每年豫东、豫中地区戏班都到此献艺，娱神娱人，百花竞放，形成了中原最大的剧种豫剧以及豫剧祥符调。清朝末年因黄河漫溢，运粮河泥沙淤积不再通航，加上铁路交通线的兴起，朱仙镇走向衰落。

朱仙镇作为明清时期中原重要商业重镇，打破了中国古代传统里坊制，是传统商业街市形成的代表。古镇中36条街和72个胡同的名字反映了明清商业文化的繁荣，如镇内的西大街、南北兴隆街、瓷器胡同、车店街、毡房胡同等。朱仙镇自春秋时期郑国建启封城，到唐宋发展，明清达到鼎盛，留下了许多动人的历史故事，郑庄公在此开疆拓土，朱亥窃符救赵，岳飞大破金兵，明清商户云集，等等。

朱仙镇启封故园景色
Scenery of Qifeng in Zhuxian Town

镇内还保存不少具有历史文化特色的建筑，以岳飞庙、清真寺、关帝庙等最具代表性。其中朱仙镇岳飞庙为全国三大岳飞庙之一，始建于

1. Zhuxian Town

Zhuxian Town in Henan Province is one of the second batch of famous historical and cultural towns published by the state. It is located about 20 kilometers to the south of Kaifeng City, Henan Province. During the Ming and Qing Dynasties, Zhuxian Town, Foshan Town, Jingde Town and Hankou Town were known as the four famous towns in China. Zhuxian Town is rich in historical heritage and historical sites. Currently, there are three national cultural heritage sites and two provincial cultural heritage sites. Zhuxian Town got its name from the fief of Zhu Hai, a famous scholar in the Warring States Period. He was a hermit and became famous for helping Lord Xinling steal the talisman to save the state of Zhao. During the Ming and Qing Dynasties, Zhuxian Town was an important hub for land and water transportation service in the Central Plains. The grain transporting river ran through the city from north to south and directly led to the Yangtze River and the Huaihe River. There were many wharves on both sides of the river, and business was busy with more than 200 ships coming and going every day, a population of hundreds of thousands. At that time, there were more than 110 temples in the town and 11 theatrical buildings, of which the theatrical building of the Ming Palace was the most important. Every year, theatrical troupes from eastern and central Henan performed here to entertain gods and people, competed. The largest opera in the Central Plains, Henan opera and Xiangfudiao (a school of Henan opera) were formed. At the end of the Qing Dynasty, Zhuxian Town declined due to the overflow of the Yellow River, the siltation of the grain transporting river and the rise of railway lines.

As an important commercial town in the Central Plains during the Ming and Qing Dynasties, Zhuxian Town broke the traditional Lifang unit system in ancient China and was the representative of traditional commercial street markets. The names of 36 streets and 72 hutongs in the ancient town reflected the prosperity of the commercial culture of the Ming and Qing Dynasties, such as the West Street, the South and North Xinglong Street, the Porcelain Hutong, the Chedian Street, the Yurt Hutong, etc. Zhuxian Town developed from the founding of Qifeng City of Zheng State in the Spring and Autumn Period to the Tang and Song Dynasties. It reached its peak in the Ming and Qing Dynasties, leaving many moving historical stories. It's the place where Duke Zheng

明成化十四年（1478），为纪念南宋名将岳飞曾经北伐在此地取得朱仙镇大捷。岳飞庙面积10500多平方米，由东西两个院落组成，有各种殿房40余间，雕梁画栋，古色古香。西院为岳飞庙的主体院落，西院为三进院，坐北朝南，依次建有山门、拜殿、大殿、寝殿，两侧由东西厢房、五子祠、五将祠等建筑群组成。在山门前有秦桧等五个奸臣的赤上身铁跪像，供世人唾弃。东院为岳飞庙碑林，有300多块石碑组成的碑林，是古代书法艺术的宝库。

朱仙镇岳飞庙
Yuefei Temple in Zhuxian Town

朱仙镇内还有启封古城遗址、岳飞点将台、韩世忠墓、运粮河故道、大石桥、朱仙镇古战场等历史遗迹。镇内还新建了启封故园、朱仙镇木版年画博物馆等旅游景点。朱仙镇不但历史文物遗迹众多，还有丰富的非物质文化遗产，其中包括国家级非物质文化遗产项目朱仙镇木版年画、豫剧祥符调等。朱仙镇是中国木版年画的发源地，兴起于唐宋，鼎盛于

expanded territory, Zhu Hai stole talismans to save Zhao State, Yue Fei defeated the Jin Army, and merchants gathered in the Ming and Qing Dynasties, and so on.

Many buildings with historical and cultural characteristics are preserved in the town, including Yuefei Temple, Mosque and Guandi Temple. Among them, Yuefei Temple in Zhuxian Town is one of the three largest Yuefei Temples in China. It was built in the 14th year of Chenghua of the Ming Dynasty (1478) to commemorate the great victory of Yuefei, a famous general of the Southern Song Dynasty, in Zhuxian Town during the northern expedition. Yuefei Temple, covering an area of more than 10500 square meters, consists of two courtyards in the east and the west. There are more than 40 halls and rooms with carved beams and painted buildings, which are antique. The west courtyard is the main courtyard of Yuefei Temple. The west courtyard is a three-entry courtyard, facing south from the north. It has a gate, a worship hall, a main hall, and a dormitory hall. On both sides stand east and west wings, Five Sons' Ancestral Hall, Five Generals' Ancestral Hall and other buildings. In front of the mountain gate, there are iron kneeling statues of five treacherous ministers including Qin Hui, all of whom are cast aside by the world. The east courtyard is the forest of steles. There are more than three hundred stone tablets in the east courtyard, which is a treasure house of ancient calligraphy art.

There are historical sites in Zhuxian Town, such as the ruins of the ancient City of Qifeng, Yuefei's commanding platform, the tomb of Han Shizhong, the old course of grain transporting river, Great Stone Bridge, the ancient battlefield of Zhuxian Town, and so on. There are also new tourist attractions in the town, such as the site of Qifeng and the Museum of Woodcut New Year Pictures in Zhuxian Town. Zhuxian Town is not only rich in historical relics, but also rich in intangible cultural heritage, including the national intangible cultural heritage project: Zhuxian Town Woodcut New Year Pictures, Xiangfudiao (a school of Henan opera), etc. Zhuxian Town is the birthplace of Chinese Woodcut New Year Pictures. It rose in the Tang and Song Dynasties, flourished in the Ming and Qing dynasties. At its peak, there were dozens of Woodcut New Year Picture shops with annual sales of millions of pieces, which were sold in several provinces in the north. There are many door gods in Zhuxian Town Woodcut New Year Pictures, with full composition, strong lines and five colors. Opera stories and

明清，高峰时有木版年画商铺数十家，年销量在几百万张，行销北方数省。朱仙镇木版年画中门神造型众多，构图饱满，线条刚劲，五色相间，戏曲故事和历史故事融入其中，内涵丰富。

朱仙镇木版年画
The Zhuxian Town Woodcut New Year Picture

2. 赊店镇

赊店镇位于河南南阳，是社旗县的政治、经济、文化中心，有潘、赵二河交汇于此，三面环水，在水运盛行的清代，这里为水旱码头，南船北马，百货流通，为清代河南四大名镇之一。这里为中原和江南数省货物集散之商埠，鼎盛时期，镇内流动人口达10余万。据南阳县志记载，赊店为豫南巨镇，500多商号总集百货，72街道分行划市，21家骡马店朝夕客商不断，48家过载行日夜装卸不停，可谓是"白日千帆过，夜间万盏灯"。赊店镇镇名相传与东汉光武帝刘秀有关，刘秀起兵时在此地赊账，并借店家"刘记"的旗子作为军旗，等到起兵成功称帝后才想起自己所赊的旗子，因此将这里命名为赊店镇。

Chapter 4 Architectural Folklore

historical stories are integrated into them with rich connotations.

2. Shedian Town

Located in Nanyang, Henan Province, Shedian Town is the political, economic and cultural center of Sheqi County, Panhe River and Zhaohe River meeting here, surrounded by water on three sides. In the Qing Dynasty, when water transportation was popular, it was one of the four famous towns in Henan Province and the strategic passage of north and south with docks for land and water transport service, and merchandise circulating. It was a commercial port for the distribution of goods in the Central Plains and several provinces south of the Yangtze River. During its heyday, the floating population in the town reached more than 100000. According to the records of Nanyang County annals, Shedian Town is an important town in southern Henan, with more than 500

赊店镇
Shedian Town

赊店镇内有远近闻名的山陕会馆，始建于乾隆二十一年（1756），历经六帝 136 年营建，规模宏大，现存建筑 152 间。晋陕两省商人多发迹于此，商会捐银数万两，遂建成了堪称一绝的山陕会馆。馆内供奉关公，是一座商业会馆类建筑与关帝庙建筑完美结合的古建筑群。整体建筑分前、中、后院落，为左右对称结构，位于中轴线上的建筑有琉璃照壁、悬鉴楼、石牌坊、大拜殿、春秋楼，两侧有配殿。关公祖籍山西，以忠义而闻名，又是商人信奉的武财神，所以山西商人多修建关帝庙以护佑其生意兴隆。

镇内还有一座保存完整的明清火神庙建筑，占地 2890 平方米，沿中轴线有山门、戏楼、木牌楼、月台、拜殿、座殿，灰砖青瓦、斗拱飞檐，整体建筑古朴雄伟，反映了当地火神信仰的盛行。镇内还有长 300 多米的南北瓷器街，是中原地区保存最为完整的明清一条街，居镇内 72 街之首，曾以经营全国各类瓷器而闻名遐迩。赊店镇还以产酒而闻名，相传东汉光武帝刘秀起兵前就在此畅饮美酒，赊店老酒享誉全国。

赊店镇山陕会馆
Shanshan Guild Hall in Shedian Town

firms, 72 streets, 21 mule and horse stores constantly attracting customers day and night, and 48 overload shops loading and unloading day and night, which can be described as "Thousands of sails in the daytime and thousands of lights at night". According to legends, the name of the town is related to Liu Xiu, Emperor Guangwu of the Eastern Han Dynasty. When Liu Xiu rose in revolt, he took credit here and borrowed the flag of the store owner "Liu Ji" as the military flag. After he succeeded and became emperor, Liu Xiu remembered the flag he had taken credit for. Therefore, he named it Shedian Town (the town of credit.)

There is a famous Shanshan guild hall in Shedian Town. It was built in 1756, the 21st year of Qianlong's reign. It has been built by six emperors for 136 years. It is large scale, with 152 buildings existing. Many businessmen from Shanxi and Shaanxi provinces made their fortune here. The chamber of Commerce donated tens of thousands of liang silver, so that a unique Shanshan guild hall was built. Guan Gong is enshrined in it. It is an ancient building complex that perfectly combines commercial guild hall buildings with Guandi Temple buildings. The whole building is divided into front, middle and rear courtyards, which is a left-right symmetrical structure. The buildings located on the central axis are glazed screen walls, Xuanjian Lou, Shipai Lou, Dabai Dian, and Chunqiu Lou, with side halls on both sides. Guan Gong, whose ancestral home is Shanxi, is famous for his loyalty and righteousness. He is also the God of wealth worshipped by businessmen. Therefore, Shanxi businessmen often build Guandi temples to bless their business prosperity.

There is also a well-preserved temple of fire of the Ming and Qing Dynasties in the town, covering an area of 2890 square meters. Along the central axis, there are gates, theatres, wooden archways, platforms, worship halls, halls, grey bricks, green tiles, brackets and cornices. The overall building is simple and magnificent, reflecting the popularity of the belief in the god of fire. There is also a porcelain street with a length of more than 300 meters from south to north. It is the best preserved street of the Ming and Qing Dynasties in the Central Plains, ranking first of the 72 streets in the town. It was famous for dealing in all kinds of porcelain in the country. The Shedian Town is also famous for producing wine. It is said that Liu Xiu, Emperor Guangwu of the Eastern Han Dynasty, drank wine here before he rose in arm. The old wine in Shedian Town is well-known all over the country.

四、中原都城

　　城市是比村、镇更为高级的聚居形式。手工业和商业从农业、畜牧业中分化出来，居民点也出现了分化，形成了以农业为主的农村和以手工业、商业为主的城市，不过早期城市内还会保留一定的农业生产，这从偃师二里头遗址、郑州商城遗址等可以看出。早期城市的出现也意味着阶层划分更为显著，掌握政权和祭祀权的贵族往往居住在城市中，甚至出现了具有相当规模的宫殿建筑，其规模、高度、形制都高于平民和奴隶。中原在中国历史上建立都城不仅很早，而且持续时间很长，充分体现出古人"择中而居"的观念。这些都城为满足人的政治、经济、文化等需要而建立，具有深厚的人文内涵。

　　中原地处黄河冲积平原，农业发达，城市出现时间很早，是夏商周三代及史前部落频繁建都之地，在中原有许多著名的中华文明探源考古都城所在地，在中国都城发展史上具有划时代的意义。譬如 2020 年中国十大考古发现之一双槐树遗址位于河南郑州市巩义黄河南岸 2000 米处，是河洛文化中心区，遗址东西长约 1500 米，南北宽约 780 米，距今 5300 年前后，是黄河流域仰韶文化中晚期发现的规格最高的具有都邑性质的中心聚落，被专家学者称为"早期中华文明的胚胎""河洛古国"，与史书中黄帝诞生的年代接近。遗址被三重环壕围绕，形成严密的防御体系，具有最早瓮城结构的围墙，封闭式排状布局的大型中心居址、采用排版筑法夯筑而成的大型连片块状夯土遗迹。这些表明中原地区很早就已经掌握了版筑夯土建城的技术，并有相当规模的人口来完成这一浩大工程。大型中心居住遗址位于内环壕的北部正中，这有可能反映出古人"择中而居，坐北朝南"的居住观念，这种建城观念影响后世几千年。该遗址位于黄河和河洛交汇处，显示出古代都城临河而居的观念，以及先民对河洛地区的高度重视，将其视为掌管四方的中枢之地。

IV. Capital Cities in the Central Plains

Cities are more advanced forms of settlement than villages and towns. Handicraft industry and commerce have been differentiated from agriculture and animal husbandry, and residential areas have also been differentiated. Rural areas dominated by agriculture and cities dominated by handicraft industry and commerce have been formed. However, some agricultural production remained in the early cities, as can be seen from the Erlitou Site in Yanshi and the Site of Shangcheng Ruins in Zhengzhou. The appearance of the early cities also meant that the class division was more obvious. The nobles who held the power and the right of sacrifice often lived in cities, and there were palace buildings of considerable scale, whose scale, height and shape were higher than those of civilians and slaves. The establishment of the capital in the Central Plains in Chinese history was not only very early, but also lasted for a long time, which fully reflected the ancient concept of "Choosing the middle to inhabit". These capitals (cities) were built to meet people's political, economic and cultural needs, and had profound humanistic connotations.

The Central Plains are located in the alluvial plain of the Yellow River, with developed agriculture. Cities appeared very early. It was the place where the Xia, Shang and Zhou Dynasties and prehistoric tribes frequently established their capitals. There are many famous archaeological capitals of Chinese civilization in the Central Plains, which is of epoch-making significance in the history of Chinese capitals. For example, Shuanghuaishu Site, one of the top ten archaeological discoveries in China in 2020, is located 2000 meters away from the south bank of the Yellow River in Gongyi, Zhengzhou City, Henan Province. It is the central area of Heluo Culture. About 1500 meters long from east to west and 780 meters wide from south to north, dating back to around 5300 years ago, the site is a central settlement with the highest specification and the nature of a city found in the middle and late Yangshao Culture in the Yellow River area. It is called "The embryo of early Chinese civilization" and "Ancient country of Heluo" by experts and scholars. It is close to the time when the Yellow Emperor was born in the history books. The site is surrounded by triple ring trenches, forming a tight

这与"黄帝四面而居其中"的神话相契合,而双槐树遗址恰与史书中记载 5000 年前黄帝文明的时代相接近,将中原作为"天地之中",将中岳嵩山视为天地中心柱,在此建都可以掌控四方九州是中国很古老的一种神圣空间观念。

巩义双槐树遗址
Shuanghuaishu Site in Gongyi

中原地区都城的营建时间早,朝代众多,历时久远,充分体现了古人"择中而居"的观念。在西周青铜器"何尊"上出现"宅兹中国"的铭文,这是"中国"最早的文字记载,这里的"中国"乃天下中心之意,记录了周成王和周公在天下中心地区营造洛邑的历史。在黄河中下游的中原建造都城,能够坐镇中州,通达九州,便于政令传达与权力渗透。在上古时期,先民便有了"象天设都"的信仰观念,认为在斗转星移的时空流转中,天上唯有北极星岿然不动,众星拱之,被视为"帝星"。而皇帝建都之所也需效法上天,建于地之中心,这样形成四方对中央的

defense system. It is a large central residential site with the walls of the earliest urn structure, closed row layout, and it is a large continuous block rammed by the layout method. These indicate that the Central Plains region has mastered the technology of building cities with rammed earth for a long time, and has a considerable population to complete this huge project. The large-scale central residential site is located in the North Center of the inner ring trench, which may reflect the ancient people's living concept of "Choosing the middle to inhabit and facing the South", which has influenced future generations for thousands of years. The site is located at the intersection of the Yellow River and the River Luo, which shows the concept that capital should be built near the river and the great importance attached by the ancestors to He Luo area, which is regarded as the central place in charge of the four directions. This is consistent with the myth that the "Yellow Emperor lived in the center". The time of Shuanghuaishu Site is close to the era of the Yellow Emperor civilization recorded in historical books 5000 years ago. Taking the Central Plains as the "Center of heaven and earth", and Mount Song as the central pillar of heaven and earth, where the capital can control the four directions and nine prefectures, is a very ancient sacred space concept in China.

The capital city in the Central Plains was built early, with numerous dynasties and a long history, which fully reflected the ancients' concept of "Choosing the middle and living in it". On the bronze ware "He Zun" of the Western Zhou Dynasty appears the inscription "Zhaizi China", which is the earliest written record of "China". Here, "China" means the center of the world. This inscription records the history of the construction of Luoyi (today's Luoyang) by King Cheng and Duke Zhou in the center of the world. By building the capital in the Central Plains of the middle and lower reaches of the Yellow River, the king could sit in Zhongzhou and reach nine prefectures, which facilitated the transmission of political orders and infiltration of power. In ancient times, the ancestors held the belief that "The emperor should set a capital as the heaven did". They believed that in the change of time and space, only the North Star stood firm in the sky and was surrounded by other stars. Thus, it was regarded as the "Emperor Star". The emperor should follow the example of heaven, building his capital in the center of the earth, so that the four sides could defend the center. Therefore, the Central

拱卫之势，因而中原地区便是理想的建都之地。

中原都城中宫殿建筑注重左右对称，"前朝后寝、左祖右社"的格局对历代都城建设影响深远，有诸多历史之最。洛阳、安阳等发掘出的宫殿遗址大都保留了坐北朝南，前为朝堂，后为寝宫，东为祖庙，西为社稷的格局，影响到汉唐长安和明清北京城的建设格局。除仰韶文化中晚期的"河洛古国"都城，中原地区还有距今4000多年龙山文化时期的淮阳平粮台遗址，考古挖掘出中国最早的城市中轴线和陶制的地下排水管道，这种对称式城市建筑格局与后代都城一脉相承。中原地区还有被学术界认为是夏朝最早都城阳城的登封王城岗遗址和考古学界影响巨大的偃师二里头遗址，发现了迄今为止中国最早的多院落大型宫室建筑遗址，开创了中国古代宫殿建筑的先河。继夏朝定鼎中原之后，商周以及之后的封建王朝也多在中原地区建都，使中原在相当长时间内成为中国的政治、经济、文化中心。在学术界评选出的中国"八大古都"之中，有半数都在中原地区，包括郑州、洛阳、安阳、开封这四个建都朝代多、规模宏大、影响深远的都市。

1. 郑州

郑州地处中原之中，自古中天下而立，除了因全国重要铁路枢纽而著名，还是国家历史文化名城。距今8000年的新郑裴李岗先民已开始在此定居从事农业生产；距今约5000年，黄帝在此诞生并建都，发明创造灿烂的文明，成为炎黄文化的肇始之地；公元前2070年，禹建立夏朝，建都阳城，而登封王城岗遗址被认为是夏都阳城；公元前1600年，商汤灭夏，建立都城亳，学界多认为其都城便是郑州商城遗址。考古界在郑州市区内发现了7000米长的黄土夯筑的城墙，围着300万平方米的城池，城中有宏大的宫殿和宗庙遗迹，城外还有防御功能的外城，城内发掘出青铜大鼎以及多处大型青铜冶炼、制陶、制骨作坊遗址，根据碳14测定年代为公元前1600年左右，是商朝初期的都城，其规模宏大，

Plains is the ideal place to build the capital.

The palace buildings in the capital of the Central Plains attached importance to symmetry. "The court was in the front, the sleeping palace was in the back, the ancestral temple was to the left and the imperial divine temple was to the right." This pattern exerted a profound impact on the construction of the capitals in later dynasties and created many records in the history. Most of the palace sites excavated in Luoyang and Anyang, sitting in the north and facing south, retained this pattern, which influenced the construction of Chang' an in the Han and Tang Dynasties and Beijing in the Ming and Qing Dynasties. In addition to the capital of "Heluo Ancient Country" in the middle and late period of Yangshao Culture, there is also the Huaiyang Pingliangtai Site in the Central Plains, which dates to Longshan Culture Period that is more than 4000 years ago. In Pingliangtai Site, archaeological excavations uncovered China's earliest urban central axis and earthenware underground drainage pipes. This symmetrical urban construction pattern is in line with the subsequent capital cities. In the Central Plains, there are also the Wangchenggang Site in Dengfeng, which is considered by the academic community to be the earliest capital of the Xia Dynasty, and the Erlitou Site in Yanshi, which has great influence in the archaeological circle. In Erlitou, so far China's earliest large-scale multi-courtyard palace building site has been uncovered, creating a precedent for ancient palace architecture in China. After the Xia Dynasty set its capital in the Central Plains, the Shang and Zhou Dynasties and later feudal dynasties also established their capitals in the Central Plains, making it the political, economic and cultural center of China for a long time. Among the "Eight Ancient Capitals" selected by the academic community, half of them are in the Central Plains. Respectively, they are Zhengzhou, Luoyang, Anyang and Kaifeng. These four large-scale cities are the capitals of many dynasties and have far-reaching influence.

1. Zhengzhou

Located in the middle of the Central Plains, Zhengzhou has been regarded as the center of the world since ancient times. It's famous not only as an important railway hub but also for its history and culture. 8000 years ago, the ancestors of Peiligang in Xinzheng (part of Zhengzhou) began to settle here and engage in

布局严密,为当时世界所罕见。郑州商城共出土了10000余件珍贵文物,其中著名的有杜岭方鼎和中国最早的原始瓷尊等。

  周朝时期,诸多方国分封于此,如祭国、管国等,至今还保留祭城、管城等地名。春秋战国时期,郑国和韩国在此争霸中原,郑庄公与周王室作战、子产改革、韩国灭郑等都发生于此。郑韩故城郑伯墓出土的两件大型青铜莲鹤方壶,造型优美,技艺绝伦,分别为国家博物馆和河南博物院的镇馆之宝。此外,郑州著名建筑还有中国功夫发源地和禅宗圣

河南博物院

Henan Museum

Chapter 4 Architectural Folklore

郑州商代遗址
Zhengzhou Shang Dynasty Site

agricultural production. About 5000 years ago, the Yellow Emperor was born in Xinzheng and established the capital here, which created a splendid civilization and became the birthplace of Yan and Huang Culture. In 2070 BC, Yu established the Xia Dynasty and set the capital in Yangcheng. The Wangchenggang Site in Dengfeng (part of Zhengzhou) is considered to be Yangcheng. In 1600 BC, the Shang Tang Dynasty destroyed the Xia Dynasty and established the capital in Bo. Many scholars believe that Bo is today's Zhengzhou Shang City Site. Archaeologists found a 7000-meter-long loess rammed wall in the urban area of Zhengzhou, enclosing a city of 3 million square meters. There were ruins of grand palaces and ancestral temples in the city, and there was also an outer city with defensive function. Bronze tripods and many large-scale sites of bronze metallurgy, pottery making and bone making workshops were excavated in the city. According to Carbon 14 dating method, these sites trace back to about 1600 BC, which corresponds to the early period of Shang Dynasty. The city was grand, and the layout was well designed, which was rare in the world at that time. More than 10 thousand precious cultural relics have been unearthed in Shang City Site, including the famous Du Ling square tripod and the earliest Primitive Porcelain Statue in China.

During the Zhou Dynasty, many states were enfeoffed here, such as the Zha

第四章 建筑民俗

河南博物院藏莲鹤方壶
The Bronze Rectangular Pot with Lotus and Crane Decorations in Henan Museum

地少林寺,以及嵩阳书院、观星台、嵩岳塔、巩义石窟寺、康百万庄园等。

2. 洛阳

洛阳是河洛文化的起源地,在古代被誉为"天下之中",自夏朝开始有10多个朝代在此建都,也正是古代文献所记载"帝王所都为中,故曰中国"。洛阳地处洛阳盆地,气候温和,土地肥沃,河洛在此交汇,水源充足,位于黄土高原和华北平原交接地带,适宜人类居住。在此建都,能够西控关中平原,东连黄淮平原,为交通要冲,有关隘和黄

State and the Guan State. So far, the names of Zhacheng and Guancheng are still preserved. During the Spring and Autumn Period and the Warring States Period, the Zheng State and the Han State competed for hegemony in the Central Plains. The war between the Duke of Zheng Zhuang and the royal family of Zhou, the reform advocated by Zichan, and the destruction of the Zheng State by the Han State all took place here. The two large bronze rectangular pots with lotus and crane decorations unearthed from Zheng Bo's tomb in the ancient city of the Zheng State are exquisite in shape and superb in craftsmanship. They are the treasures of the National Museum and the Henan Museum respectively. In addition, famous buildings in Zhengzhou include Shaolin Temple, the birthplace of Chinese Kung Fu and the holy land of Zen, as well as Songyang Academy, Star Observation Terrace, Songyue Pagoda, Gongyi Grotto Temple and KANGBAI-WANS Mansions and so on.

少林寺
Shaolin Temple

2. Luoyang

Luoyang, the birthplace of Heluo Culture, was known as "The center of the world" in ancient times. Since the Xia Dynasty, more than 10 dynasties have established their capitals here, which exactly illustrates what the ancient literature

河为屏障，易守难攻，故此先后有夏、商、东周、东汉、曹魏、西晋、北魏、隋、唐、武周、西周、后梁、后唐、后晋等在此建都。二里头遗址、两周洛邑遗址、东汉都城遗址等都依稀可见洛阳作为都城的恢宏大气。

　　洛阳作为千年帝都，历史上园林众多，景色秀丽，以牡丹最为著名，"花开时节动京城"，有"洛阳牡丹甲天下"的美誉。至今每年四月在洛阳都会举行盛大的牡丹花会，吸引着海内外的游客前来赏牡丹游古都。洛阳举世闻名的名胜古迹还有中国第一座汉传佛寺白马寺，以及关林、周公庙、香山寺等。而世界文化遗产龙门石窟是世界上造像最多、规模

龙门石窟

Longmen Grottoes

白马寺

The White Horse Temple

records. That is, "The place where the emperor set the capital was regarded as the center. Hence, the name China came into being". Luoyang is located in the Luoyang Basin, where the climate is mild and the land is fertile. Rivers meet here, and water is abundant. It is located at the junction of the Loess Plateau and the North China Plain, which is suitable for human habitation. Establishing the capital here can control the Guanzhong Plain in the west and the Huang Huai Plain in the east. As a traffic hub, the passes and the Yellow River constitute its barriers. As such, Luoyang is easy to defend but difficult to attack. Therefore, the Xia, Shang, Eastern Zhou, Eastern Han, Cao Wei, Western Jin, Northern Wei, Sui, Tang, Wu Zhou, Western Zhou, Later Liang, Later Tang, and Later Jin established their capitals here. Erlitou Site, Luoyi Site of Western and Eastern Zhou Dynasty, the capital site of the Eastern Han Dynasty, among others, still vaguely show the magnificence of Luoyang as a Capital.

  Luoyang, as a thousand-year-old imperial capital, boasts many gardens and beautiful scenery in history, among which peony is the most famous. "When peony is in full bloom, the whole capital is surprised with its beauty". It also enjoys the reputation of "Luoyang peony is the best in the world". Up till now, a

洛阳牡丹
Luoyang Peony

最大的石刻艺术宝库,被联合国教科文组织评为"中国石刻艺术的最高峰",石窟始凿于北魏孝文帝期间,盛于唐,终于清末,历时1400多年。在洛阳城南伊水东西两山峭壁上,绵延1000米,现存洞窟佛龛2345个,造像11余万尊。其中武则天时代雕刻的卢舍那大佛高17.14米,头高4米,耳朵长达1.9米,造型优美、气势恢宏、富有生机,是唐代雕刻艺术的最高成就,是大唐盛世的象征。

3. 安阳

安阳殷墟是商朝后期的都城,盘庚迁都于此。殷墟入选世界文化遗产名录,出土了迄今为止中国发现最早的成熟文字体系甲骨文,还有数

grand Peony Fair is held in Luoyang every April, attracting tourists from home and abroad to visit the ancient capital. Other world-famous places of interest in Luoyang include the White Horse Temple, which is the first Han Buddhist temple in China, as well as Guanlin, Zhougong Temple and Xiangshan Temple. Longmen Grottoes, a world cultural site, is the largest stone carving art treasure house with the largest number of statues in the world. It has been rated as "The Highest Peak of Chinese Stone Carving Art" by UNESCO. The grottoes were first carved during the reign of Emperor Xiaowen of the Northern Wei Dynasty, flourished in the Tang Dynasty, and completed in the late Qing Dynasty, lasting more than 1400 years. There are 2345 existing caves and shrines with more than 110,000 statues, spreading on the east and west cliffs of Yishui in the south of Luoyang City, stretching 1000 meters. Among them, the Lushena Buddha carved in the era of Empress Wu Zetian is 17.14 meters high, with a 4-meter-high head and 1.9-meter-long ears. Beautiful, magnificent and full of vitality, it is the highest achievement of the carving art in the Tang Dynasty and a symbol of the prosperity of the Tang Dynasty.

3. Anyang

Yinxu in Anyang was the capital of the late Shang Dynasty and King Pan Geng moved the capital here. Yinxu was included in the world cultural heritage list. Archeologists unearthed in Yinxu the oracle bone inscriptions which was the earliest mature writing system found in China so far. They also excavated in Yinxu a huge number of bronzes, jades and pottery, indicating the brilliant civilization of the Shang Dynasty. Through exploration and excavation, it is found that Yinxu is about 5.5 kilometers long from south to north and 6.5 kilometers long from east to west, covering a total area of about 36 square kilometers. The cultural relics in the peripheral area of Yinxu are far less dense than those in the central area. Among the cultural relics in the peripheral area, most belong to late Shang Dynasty and few belong to early Shang, indicating that the development of Yin capital is radiating from the center to the four sides, and Yin capital has been expanding over 200 years' construction. This suggests that the population of Yin capital is increasing and the scale of the city is enlarging with the needs of development. Yinxu is divided into palace and ancestral temple area, tomb area,

量巨大的青铜器、玉石器、陶器等，表明商代文明的辉煌灿烂。通过勘探和发掘，现在发现殷墟范围南北长约 5.5 千米，东西长约 6.5 千米，总面积约 36 平方千米。殷墟边缘区域的文化遗存远不如中心区域文化遗存密集，殷墟边缘的殷代文化遗存，早期的居少，晚期的居多，说明

"人工天河"红旗渠
Man-made River-Hongqiqu Canal

殷墟出土的后母戊鼎
The Houmuwu Ding Unearthed in Yinxu

civilian area and so on. The tombs are classified into the tomb of King Yin with large scale and numerous funerary objects and the tombs of nobles and civilians, showing obvious class differentiation. The Houmuwu Ding unearthed in Yinxu is 133 centimeters high and 875 kilograms in weight, making it the largest known bronze ware in the world. A large number of bronzes unearthed from Fu Hao's tomb are famous for their beautiful appearance and originality.

After the Shang Dynasty, Yedu was built here during the Cao Wei Period, which is of pioneering significance in the history of capital construction in China. In the Han Dynasty and before, the capital cities were mostly enclosed and irregularly laid out. The palaces were built on the highest place of the city, surrounded by official offices and residential areas. Yedu began to adopt a checkerboard-shaped closed layout with the central axis as the center of symmetry. The central axis of the city was also the central axis of the palace, and the palace offices and streets were symmetrically and evenly distributed along it. The palaces and official offices were concentrated in the northern part of the city, which was completely separated from the residential quarters, setting a precedent for the neat layout, rigorous structure and obvious division of the capital. Yedu had a certain

殷都发展是由中心向四边辐射延伸的，经过200多年的经营不断扩充。这能够反映出殷都人口在不断增加，城市规模随着发展需要在不断扩大。殷墟分为宫殿宗庙区、墓葬区、平民区等，而墓葬分为规模宏大、陪葬品众多的殷王陵和贵族平民墓葬，显示出明显的阶层分化。在殷墟出土的后母戊鼎，鼎高133厘米，重达875千克，是目前已知世界上最大的青铜器。妇好墓出土的大量青铜器以造型美观、独具匠心而著称。

商朝之后，曹魏时期又在此建邺都，在我国都城建设史上具有开创意义。在两汉及以前都城大都是封闭式不规则布局，宫殿建在城中制高点上，周围散布官署和居民区。而邺都开始采用以中轴为中心对称的棋盘形封闭式布局，城市中轴线同时也是王宫的中轴线，宫殿官署和街道里坊都依它为对称均匀分布。宫殿和官署集中在城市北部，与居民里坊截然分开，开创了都城规划布局整齐、结构严谨、区分明显的先例，对后世都城建设如隋唐长安、明清北京等都有一定影响。南北朝十六国时期，邺都又先后作为后赵、冉魏、前燕的都城，是民族融合的中心。除了世界文化遗产殷墟，安阳的著名建筑还有汤阴岳飞庙，为全国三大岳飞庙之一。安阳还有被誉为"人工天河"的红旗渠，于20世纪60年代历时10年建成，在当时缺乏机械设备的条件下依靠人力在太行山上开凿出70余千米长的总干渠以及数百千米的配套支渠，解决了当地山区干旱缺水的问题。

汤阴岳飞庙
Yuefei Temple in Tangyin

impact on the construction of later capitals, such as Chang'an in the Sui and Tang Dynasties and Beijing in the Ming and Qing Dynasties. During the sixteen Kingdoms Period of the Northern and Southern Dynasties, Yedu was successively the capital of later Zhao, Ran Wei and Former Yan, and was the center of national integration. In addition to Yinxu, a world cultural heritage, the famous building in Anyang also includes Yuefei Temple in Tangyin, which is one of the three Yuefei Temples in China. Anyang also boasts the Red Flag Canal, known as the "Artificial River in The Sky", which took 10 years to complete in the 1960s. Under the condition of lack of mechanical equipment at that time, local people dug more than 70 kilometers of main stretch of the canal and hundreds of kilometers of supporting branches on the Taihang Mountain on their own, solving the problem of drought and water shortage in the local mountainous areas.

第四章　建筑民俗

安阳殷墟
Yinxu in Anyang

清明上河图（局部）
Along the River During the Qingming Festival (A Section of the Painting)

4. Kaifeng

Kaifeng has been the capital of Xia Dynasty, the State of Wei in the Warring States Period, the State of Liang in Western Han Dynasty, Later Liang, Later Jin, Later Han and Later Zhou Dynasties in the Five Dynasties Period, Northern Song and Jin Dynasties in history. It is an ancient city with a history of more than 3,000 years, and it is also the prosperous Dongjing Bianliang [1], captured in a famous painting named "Along the River During the Qingming Festival" (or "Qingming Shanghe Tu" in Chinese). There are few materials excavated in Laoqiu, the capital of Xia Dynasty. During the Spring and Autumn Period, the state of Zheng built a city named "Qifeng" here. During the Warring States Period, King Wei Hui moved his capital here and named it Daliang. It developed into a large-scale city. According to historical records, there were 13 gates in Daliang City, and 300 thousand troops were needed to defend the city during the war. Daliang City could be divided into a small town and a big town. The small town was located in the northwest of the big town. In the small town, there were towering palaces as well as high platforms and gardens specially for princes and nobles. Many historical stories took place in Daliang City, for example, King Xin Ling of the state of Wei stealing talisman to save Zhao, surrounding Wei to save Zhao, Mencius seeing King Liang Hui, and so on. After the Tang Dynasty, Chang'an and Luoyang were seriously damaged by the war, and the political center moved eastward. Kaifeng, as an important hub of canal and land transportation, was called "Dongjing" when it served as the capital of the Later Liang Dynasty, the Later Jin Dynasty, the Later Han Dynasty and the Later Zhou Dynasty successively. The City of Kaifeng was expanded, and the waterway outside Kaifeng was dredged, so that Bian River could reach Huaihe River directly.

By the Northern Song Dynasty, Kaifeng, as a capital which had witnessed 9 Emperors and lasted 168 years, had become the political, economic and cultural center of the country. It was the most populous and economically and culturally developed city in the world. Thus, historically it was known as "Bianjing, the most magnificent city in the world". The capital city of the Northern Song Dynasty

---

[1] Bianliang, today's Kaifeng, was called Dongjing in the Five Dynasties and Ten Kingdoms and the Northern Song Dynasty.

4. 开封

开封，历史上曾有夏、战国魏、西汉梁国、五代梁晋汉周、北宋、金等在此建都，是一座具有 3000 多年建成史的古都，是《清明上河图》中繁华富丽的东京汴梁。夏都老丘现在发掘的资料较少，春秋时期郑国在此建"启封"城。战国时期魏惠王迁都于此并取名大梁，成为一座规模宏大的城市，据史料记载大梁城有 13 个城门，在战争期间需要 30 万军队来守城。大梁城有小城和大郭之分，小城设在大郭西北，里面建有巍峨的宫殿等，还有专门供王公贵族游乐的高台和园林。魏国信陵君窃符救赵、围魏救赵、孟子见梁惠王等都发生在大梁城。唐朝之后，长安和洛阳因战争遭到严重破坏，政治中心东移，开封作为运河和陆上交通

开封铁塔
The Iron Pagoda in Kaifeng

adopted the new structure-a triple square city, which was divided into Imperial City (Palace City), Inner City and Outer City. There were 4 canals, 33 bridges and 4 imperial roads in the city. An endless stream of vehicles ran on the road, and boats in the waterways were like crucian carp crossing the river. The Imperial City was located in the northwest of the central city, with a perimeter of 2.5 kilometers. There were towers at the four corners of the Imperial City, several tens of feet high and six gates. The imperial palace and the government agencies were located here. Daqing Hall, Mingtang Hall, Xuande Building were landmark buildings. The perimeter of the inner city was 12.5 kilometers and that of the outer city was 25 kilometers. The construction of Dongjing had the significance of connecting the past with the future. On the one hand, it preserved the traditional pattern that "the court was in the front, the market was in the back, the ancestral temple was to the left and the imperial divine temple was to the right". On the other hand, it broke the restrictions of the urban layout in the Sui and Tang Dynasties. In Dongjing, the palaces were built in the center of the city. There were strict requirements about the central axis of the palaces, the imperial roads and the central axis of the Imperial City. This layout was later inherited by the Jin people, followed by the Yuan Dynasty when the capital was built. When the Ming and Qing Dynasties built Beijing and the Forbidden City, they also adopted this layout.

The biggest breakthrough of Dongjing in the history of the capital city was to remove the restrictions of urban planning in the past. Business and residential areas were no longer separated. Commerce and handicraft industry were all over the city, which promoted the prosperity of the commodity economy and the vitality of the city. Bustling night markets and street markets appeared. There were many specialized markets, restaurants, tea houses, Wazi (a place for amusement), and handicraft workshops in Dongjing. The citizen economy and culture began to rise. Entertainment activities such as singing, storytelling, shadow puppetry and acrobatics became popular. In addition to the political function, the economic and cultural functions of the capital had been significantly enhanced. In order to meet the needs of the new capital's development, Dongjing had many perfect mechanisms in its urban management. It implemented the system of Xiangfang (the integration of business areas and residential areas), and formed a four-level management organization. It paid attention to the fire prevention facilities,

重要枢纽先后作为后梁、后晋、后汉、后周的都城,称为"东京";并对开封城市进行了扩建,疏通了开封对外的水道交通,使汴河可以直达淮河。

到北宋时期,开封作为都城历经九帝168年,成为全国政治、经济、文化中心,是世界上人口最多、经济文化最发达的城市,史称"汴京壮丽天下无"。北宋都城采用三重方城的新结构,分为皇城(宫城)、里城、外城。城内有4条运河、33座桥梁、4条御道,路上车辆络绎不绝,水道舟楫如过江之鲫。皇城位于城中央稍偏西北,周长2.5千米,城四角有城楼,高数十丈,设城门六座。城内为皇宫及中央政府机构所在,大庆殿、明堂、宣德楼等是著名建筑。里城周长12.5千米,外城周长25千米。东京城建设具有承前启后的意义,保存了我国历史上都城"前朝后市、左祖右社"的传统格局,但又打破了隋唐时期都市中坊、里的限制。将宫阙建在城市中央,对殿群的中轴线和御道与皇城的中轴线要求十分严格。这种格局后来为金人继承,元建大都时仿效,明清建北京城和紫禁城时得以延续。

东京城在都城史上最大突破在于打破原来都城的坊、里限制,市、坊不再分开,商业和手工业遍布全城,促进商品经济繁荣和城市活力,出现了繁华的夜市和街市。东京城内行市、酒楼、茶坊、瓦子、手工作坊等众多,市民经济和文化开始兴起,唱词、说书、皮影、杂技等娱乐活动流行开来。都城在政治功能基础上,经济和文化功能显著增强。为适应新的都城发展需要,东京城在城市管理方面有诸多完善机制,实行厢坊制,形成四级管理机构;注重防火设施,有军队巡逻,高处设望火楼,楼下屯兵100人,备水桶、洒子、火叉等灭火工具,由此成立了专门救火队;还有完善的供水和排水设施,宋仁宗时期东京城有水井390个,开挖排水大小水沟253条,每年二月都要清淤;还注重街道卫生,开创城市道路洒水先河,禁止侵占街道和排放污水。现在开封城内的铁塔、繁塔等依稀能看到大宋往昔的风采,清明上河园中仿佛能重温东京梦华的绚烂。

had military patrols, set up fire watchtowers at high places with 100 soldiers stationed downstairs, and prepared buckets, sprinklers, fire forks and other fire-fighting tools, so a special fire-fighting team was established. There was also perfect water supply and drainage facilities. During the reign of Renzong in Song Dynasty, there were 390 wells in Dongjing and 253 ditches were excavated. Every February, silt in the ditches was removed. Dongjing also stressed the street sanitation and sprinkled water on the city roads, which was unprecedented in history. Encroachment on the streets and discharging sewage to the streets were prohibited. Now the magnificence of the great Song Dynasty can still be vaguely seen from the Iron Pagoda and the Po Pagoda in Kaifeng City. The dreamlike splendor of Dongjing can be re-experienced in the Qingming Riverside Landscape Garden, a large theme park.

开封清明上河园景区
The Qingming Riverside Landscape Garden

第五章

民间美术

Chapter 5

Folk Art

中原地域广大，蕴藏着许多作为民族文化载体的民间工艺美术，这些丰富多彩、形式各异的乡土艺术，被专家们称为"地上的活文物"。据《东京梦华录》及有关史料记载：宋代京城，民间各种工艺作坊与规模较大的宋廷"百作"作坊交相辉映。制作、展示、出售各类民间手工艺品的店铺遍布京城，并渗透进人们的衣、食、住、行、娱诸多方面。其中相当一部分工艺品，历经千年延传至今，仍以其深厚的文化内涵丰富着人们的精神世界。研究中原民俗文化，民间工艺美术是重要的一环。我们企盼中原民间美术能成为全人类的精神财富，并不断发扬光大。

一、方城石猴

1. 方城石猴的文化背景

方城地处豫南，属南阳市管辖，其境内仰韶文化、西周文化遗址驰名中外。这里有中国现存最早的楚长城遗址，有西汉外交家张骞封侯之地博望镇，有道教炼丹升仙的胜地黄石山，有汉代张良拾履拜师、黄石公传授兵书的仙人桥。丰厚的文化积淀和博大精深的道教思想影响并构成了当地独特的民俗风情。张骞在此封侯的荣耀，拨动着人们建功立业的渴望；仙人指点的机遇，又掺杂了诸多对好运的企盼，古朴的民风孕育成简明的形象符号予以表达。

2. 方城石猴的艺术特色

方城石猴的个头虽说不大，雕刻下来却不容易。首先是选好料，石猴采用当地特产的滑石制作。选中石材后，用大砍刀劈出毛坯，再根据毛坯的天然形状，构思出适合雕刻的造型。整个造型过程不画线，不描样，没有一定之规，全靠个人丰富的想象力和用刀技巧。所以，方城的石猴各具形态，绝不雷同，凭的是艺人"眼观、心想、手到"的功夫。如果给石猴上了颜色，小猴子的表情和身体结构会更加明显、清晰、生

The vast land of the Central Plains contains many folk arts, which are the carriers of the national culture. These colorful and various local arts are called "Living cultural relics on the ground" by experts. According to *A Dream of Splendor in Dongjing* (*Dongjing Menghua Lu*) and relevant historical records, in the capital of the Song Dynasty, various folk craft workshops and the large-scale "Baizuo" workshops managed by the government complement each other. Shops that make, display and sell all kinds of folk handicrafts are all over the capital, and penetrate into many aspects of people's lives, for instance, clothing, food, housing, transportation and entertainment. A considerable number of these handicrafts have been passed down for thousands of years and still enrich people's spiritual world with their profound cultural connotation. Folk arts and crafts are an important part of the study of folk culture in the Central Plains. We hope that the folk art in the Central Plains can become the spiritual wealth of all mankind and be carried forward continuously.

I. Fangcheng Stone Monkey

1. The Cultural Background of Fangcheng Stone Monkey

Fangcheng is in the southern Henan, under the jurisdiction of Nanyang City. The Yangshao Culture and the Western Zhou Culture sites here are well-known at home and abroad. Here also exist the earliest ruins of the Great Wall of Chu in China, Bowang Town, the place where diplomat Zhang Qian was granted marquis in the Western Han Dynasty, Huangshi Mountain, a resort for Taoist alchemy and immortality, and Xianren Bridge, where Zhang Liang in the Han Dynasty picked up Huang Shigong's shoes, and later Huang Shigong taught him military strategies. The rich cultural accumulation and profound Taoist thought have influenced and formed the unique local folk customs. The glory of Zhang Qian's being conferred Marquis here inspires people to make outstanding achievements. The opportunity of being guided by a master mingles with many hopes for good luck. Primitive folk customs are expressed through concise symbols.

2. The Artistic Features of Fangcheng Stone Monkey

Although Fangcheng stone monkey is not big, it is not easy to carve. The

动，通体充满浓郁质朴的乡土味道。栩栩如生的猴子，一个个红眼睛、黑眼珠、绿鼻子，花花绿绿的颜色看上去喜庆热烈。红色是太阳的颜色，意为红红火火；绿色代表植物，寓意生机勃勃；大面积的黄色象征土地和财富，温暖而灿烂。

因"石猴"与"时候"（机遇）谐音，民间就有了"石猴到门前，四季保平安"的说法，把石猴视为"吉祥、纳福"之物。不同造型的石猴被赋予不同的寓意，如"猴背猴"为"辈辈封侯"，猴子在马上奔驰前行意思是"马上封侯"等。不光石猴的造型有吉祥的寓意，而且送给别人的石猴，还被称为送"好时候"（即好时运）。每到春节、农历三月三、九月九古刹大会，人们便争相购买、互致赠送，企盼能给自己和亲人带来好运。除了吉祥的寓意，石猴还有实用功能，石猴在墙壁、石板上一画即显，可当作粉笔用；石猴还具有消炎止血的药用价值，所以它集吉祥物、玩物和药物为一体，形象生动有趣，美观实惠，备受人们喜爱。

3. 代表性作品

民间艺人用当地的滑石雕出猴子形状后，用黄、绿、红、黑等颜料涂染勾画在石猴身上，故又称"画石猴"。

这是早期单纯自然色的石猴，造型简练，手法概括，简称"八刀猴"。

辈辈封侯

母猴怀里有只猴，背上还背着一只猴，寓意"辈辈封侯"。由于它独特的造型和吉祥的谐

小石猴
A Small Stone Monkey

first step is to choose the right material. The stone monkey is made of talc, a local specialty. After selecting the material, the craftsman uses a machete to chop out the roughcast, and then conceives a shape suitable for carving. During the whole process, the craftsman does not draw lines or copy other patterns, and there are no certain rules. It all depends on the craftsman's own imagination and knife skills. Therefore, the stone monkeys in Fangcheng have different shapes, which mainly rely on the craftsman's expertise of "observing, thinking, and making". If the stone monkey is colored, its expression and body structure will become more vivid, eye-catching, and full of strong rustic flavor. The lifelike monkeys, with red eyes, black eyeballs, green noses and various colors, look festive and vibrant. Red is the color of the sun, indicating prosperity; green represents plants, implying vitality; large areas of yellow symbolize land and wealth, warm and brilliant.

Since the "stone monkey" is homophonic with "time" (opportunity), the saying that "Stone monkeys in front of the door can ensure safety in the four seasons" is popular with the local people. They regard the stone monkey as a symbol of "Auspiciousness and Blessing". Stone monkeys in different shapes are endowed with different meanings. For instance, "one monkey on the back of the other monkey" means "marquis for generations" and a monkey galloping forward on a horse means "marquis to be", etc. Not only does the shape of the stone monkey have auspicious meaning, but also the stone monkey given to others is called "Good time" (that is, good fortune). Every Spring Festival, on the third day of March and the ninth day of September in the lunar calendar, people rush to buy stone monkeys and give them to each other, hoping to bring good luck to themselves and their relatives. In addition to the auspicious implications, the stone monkeys also have practical functions. They can be used as chalks, drawing on the wall and slate. They also have the medicinal value of anti-inflammatory and hemostatic. So the stone monkeys can serve as mascots, playthings and drugs at the same time. They are vivid and interesting, beautiful and affordable; therefore, they are loved by people.

3. Representative Works

After the craftsman carves the shape of a monkey out of the local talc, he will paint it with yellow, green, red, black, and other pigments. So, the stone monkey is

音,使得它长久不衰。当地人们逢年过节以此为吉祥物让孩子佩戴,在方城县形成一种独特的"猴文化"。

猪八戒背猴
Pig Bajie Backs a Monkey

中国人历来有"讨口彩"的习惯,石猴的猴与王侯将相的侯同音,顺应了古时人们"加官封侯"的心理,又给石猴增添了一种吉祥、富贵的象征意义。猪八戒背猴寓意"一方诸侯(猪猴)"。

画石猴
Painted Stone Monkey

also called "painted stone monkey".

This is an early stone monkey with natural color, concise shape and simple technique, referred to as "Eight-Knife Monkey".

Marquis for generations

The mother monkey has a monkey in her arms and a monkey on her back, which means "Every generation is ennobled as a marquis". Because of its unique shape and auspicious homophony, it prevails for a long period of time. Local people take this as a mascot for their children to wear during festivals, forming a unique "Monkey Culture" in Fangcheng County.

Chinese people have always had the habit of "making well-wishing complementary remarks". The Chinese character " 猴 " (monkey) in the expression " 石猴 " (stone monkey) is pronounced the same as the Chinese character " 侯 " (marquis) in the expression " 王侯将相 " (kings, marquis, generals and ministers), which conforms to the ancient people's longing for " being ennobled a marquis", and adds a symbolic meaning of auspiciousness and wealth to the stone monkey. Pig Bajie's backing of a monkey signifies "A marquis governing a place (pig and monkey)".

二、虢州澄泥砚

1. 虢州澄泥砚的文化背景

虢州澄泥砚与端砚、歙砚和洮砚并称为中国四大名砚，也是黄河文化的象征。虢州地处豫西，是河洛文化和道教文化的重要发祥地域。黄河岸边的能工巧匠澄泥制砚，制作出的澄泥砚外形泽如美玉，手触生晕，坚硬如石，扣之铿然有声。又因其"积墨不腐，贮墨不耗，冬不冻，夏不枯"的独特功能，澄泥砚历来被文人墨客所珍重。虢州澄泥砚最早有明确文献记载的资料在唐代，说"唐为贡品"。宋代欧阳修、苏东坡、米芾等都有关于澄泥砚的论述，说它具有"石"之坚固，又有"泥"之独特。尤其是米芾、苏东坡视澄泥砚为至宝。到了清代，乾隆皇帝对澄泥砚的喜爱更是有过之而无不及，仅经乾隆御笔题名的澄泥砚就有30多方。

2. 虢州澄泥砚的艺术特色

上等的澄泥砚品质优良，其品质观之如碧玉，抚之如童肤，扣之若金石。颜色以鳝鱼黄为最佳，其次是绿头青、玫瑰紫、朱砂红等。澄泥砚不仅实用，而且雕工讲究。它取黄河中游的澄泥为原料，在研究继承历代制砚技术的基础上，融入了现代科技手段，推陈出新，形成了一整套独特的工艺。洛阳新安县龙砚斋制砚除了注重澄泥砚形制的多样性以外，更追求烧制过程中奇幻的窑变效果。在内容和立意上，澄泥砚既有着眼大义，以黄河文化、民族文化为背景进行设计创作的作品，也有一些侧重表现情趣的作品，使这种古老的艺术形式焕发出了新的活力。

II. Guozhou Chengni Inkstone

1. The Cultural Background of Guozhou Chengni Inkstone

Guozhou Chengni inkstone, Duan inkstone, She inkstone and Tao inkstone, are known as the four famous inkstones in China. Guozhou Chengni inkstone is a symbol of the Yellow River culture. Guozhou, located in the west of Henan Province, is an important place where Heluo Culture and Taoist Culture originated. Chengni inkstones are made of clarified fine mud by skilled craftsmen on the bank of the Yellow River. They are as lustrous as jade and as hard as stone, exhibiting a halo when touched, and sonorous when knocked. In addition, because of its unique function that "left ink will not decay, stored ink will not be consumed, ink will not freeze in winter or dry in summer", Chengni inkstones have always been cherished by literati. Guozhou Chengni inkstones were first documented in the Tang Dynasty. The record goes like this, "In the Tang dynasty, Chengni inkstone was used as a tribute". In the Song Dynasty, Ouyang xiu, Su Dongpo and Mi Fu all discussed the Chengni inkstone, saying that it had the hardness of "stone" and the uniqueness of "mud". Mi Fu and Su Dongpo even regarded it as a treasure. In the Qing Dynasty, Emperor Qian Long was even more fond of it. There were more than 30 Chengni inkstones inscribed by his imperial brush.

2. The Artistic Features of Guozhou Chengni Inkstone

The prime Chengni inkstones are of high quality. They look like jasper, stroke like a child's skin and knock like a stone. The best color is eel yellow, followed by green, rose purple, cinnabar red. Chengni inkstones are not only practical, but also exquisite in carving. The craftsmen use the clarified fine mud from the middle reaches of the Yellow River as raw material. On the basis of studying and inheriting the inkstone making craft of the past, they integrate modern science and technology into it, forming a set of unique processes. While making the inkstones, Longyanzhai in Xin'an County, Luoyang, not only pays attention to the diversity of the shapes, but also pursues the fantastic kiln change effect in the firing process. In terms of Content and theme, there are both works designed and

3. 代表性作品

人马寨澄泥砚
A Chengni Inkstone of Renma Village

三门峡陕县人马寨村澄泥砚是陕州澄泥砚的发源地，当地制砚历史已有 1000 余年。人马寨的澄泥砚多是一些动物形象，如乌龟、蟾蜍等。

created with the Yellow River culture and national culture as the background, and works that focus on expressing interest, which makes this ancient art form full of new vitality.

3. Representative Works

Renmazhai Village in Shaanxian County, Sanmenxia, is the birthplace of Shanzhou Chengni inkstone. The inkstone making history there has been more than 1000 years. Chengni inkstones in Renmazhai mostly take the forms of animals, such as turtles, toads and so on.

三、濮阳麦秆画

1. 濮阳麦秆画概况

濮阳地处豫北，是我国小麦的主要产地之一。当地麦秆资源丰富，麦秆质地柔韧，光洁如玉，薄如缎带。濮阳素有捏制草辫的传统，是远近闻名的"草辫之乡"。传说东汉刘秀被王莽追杀，万般无奈，藏于麦地之中，麦草随即化为树林保护刘秀。因此当地人视麦草为祈福迎祥之草，遂制作麦草画，供奉朝廷。濮阳的能工巧匠用当地俯拾皆是的麦秆在黑色底布上贴出潇洒飘逸的花鸟图案。麦秆画和剪纸、布贴一样，是一种剪贴的艺术，它适用场所广泛，是理想的装饰艺术品，很受社会各界的欢迎。

2. 麦秆画的艺术特色

从普通的麦秆变成艺术品，中间要经过许多道工序，要融入艺术家的创造。就拿麦秆的加工来说，一般的小麦秸秆并不适合，因为秸秆长度较短。制作麦秆画所需的麦秆要秆长皮薄，柔韧性强，不易变形，容易加工。艺人会从当地数十种小麦中精选出所需的品种，把选好的麦秆剥去外衣，放在平面上开始熨烫。濮阳麦秆画一般都不着色，大多采用麦秆本身的光泽、纹彩和质感，麦秆颜色的深浅层次和熨烫的温度、力度和速度关系非常密切。麦秆熨烫好后，就可以根据作品的需要进行剪裁和粘贴了。做好的麦秆画人物图案舒展自如，姿态神情生动逼真，光泽透亮，艺术感染力很强。如果不知底细，人们还真不知道这些工艺精湛的艺术品是用小麦的秸秆做成的。濮阳麦秆画各种题材都能表现，亭台楼阁、高山飞瀑、鸟兽虫鱼、天上人间，制作麦秆画的厂家和个人都有自己独特的绝活。《反弹琵琶》《〈水浒〉系列人物》《虢国夫人游春图》等麦秆画品种，很受国内外人士的欢迎。许多外国朋友到濮阳看了麦秆

III. Puyang Wheat Straw Painting

1. An Overview of Puyang Wheat Straw Painting

Puyang, located in the north of Henan Province, is one of the main wheat production areas in China. The wheat straw resources there are rich, and the straw texture is flexible, as smooth as jade, and as thin as satin ribbon. Puyang has the tradition of plaiting straw and is known as the "Hometown of straw plaits" far and near. Legend has it that Liu Xiu was hunted down by Wang Mang in the Eastern Han Dynasty. He was helpless and hid himself in the wheat field. The wheat straws immediately turned into a forest to protect him. Therefore, the local people regarded wheat straw as the grass for blessing and auspiciousness. They made wheat straw paintings and gave them to the imperial court as tributes. The craftsmen in Puyang create the elegant patterns of flowers and birds on the black cloth with local wheat straws that can be found everywhere. Wheat straw painting, like paper cutting and cloth pasting, is a kind of art of cutting and pasting. It is suitable for a wide range of places. As an ideal decorative art, wheat straw painting is very popular with people from all walks of life.

2. The Artistic Features of Wheat Straw Painting

From ordinary wheat straw to artwork, there are many processes into which artists' creation must be integrated. Take the processing of wheat straw for example. Ordinary wheat straw is not suitable, because it is short. The straw needed for making straw paintings should be long and thin, with strong flexibility, not easy to deform and easy to process. The artist will select the desired one from dozens of local wheat varieties, peel off the selected straw, put it on a flat surface and start ironing. Puyang wheat straw paintings are generally not colored. Most of them use the luster, vein and texture of the straw itself. The depth of straw color is closely related to the temperature, strength and speed of ironing. Once ironed, the straw can be cut and pasted according to the needs of the work. The characters in the well-made wheat straw paintings are natural, vivid, translucent, and artistically appealing. Without background knowledge, perhaps people really don't know that these exquisite works of art are made of wheat straw. Puyang wheat straw paintings can

画之后，不禁称奇叫好，赞扬它："濮阳麦秆画，中华又一绝。"

从审美上来说，以黑色为底色是麦秆画一个重要的美学特征。濮阳麦秆画大多在黑底色上粘贴出彩色的图案，黑色常常有助于相配色彩的风格展示。从工艺上来说，与其他地区的麦秆画相比，濮阳麦秆画以做工精细见长。尤其擅长毛刺工艺，并以此为特色，追求细腻、生动、逼真的风格。在造型上，濮阳麦秆画吸收了国画、剪纸、刺绣、雕刻等多种表现手法，用简明线条将繁杂的事物表现得淋漓尽致，风格古朴自然、典雅大方。

3. 麦秆画作品赏析

虢国夫人游春图（聂远征）
Painting of Lady of Guoguo on a Spring Outing (Created by Nie Yuanzheng)

聂远征是麦秆画国家级非物质文化遗产代表性传承人，其家族自明朝宣德年间就开始从事麦秆画的制作，传承发展至今已有几百年的历史。

迎春花和大公鸡组合在一起构图，"鸡"与"吉"谐音，画面寓意"迎春大吉"。

"四君子"是中国传统文化的题材，它们分别是指梅花、兰花、翠竹和菊花，代表的品质分别是傲、幽、淡、逸，成为中国人借物喻志的象征。

express a variety of themes, such as pavilions, mountains, waterfalls, birds, animals, insects, fish, heaven and earth. Manufacturers and individuals who make wheat straw paintings have their own unique skills. Famous works like *Playing the Pipa Behind the Back*, the series of characters in the novel *Water Margin*, and *Painting of Lady of Guoguo on a Spring Outing* are very popular at home and abroad. After seeing the wheat straw paintings in Puyang, many foreign friends couldn't help acclaiming: "Puyang wheat straw painting is another unique feature of China."

Aesthetically speaking, using black as the background color is an important aesthetic feature of wheat straw paintings. Puyang straw paintings are mostly pasted with colorful patterns on a black background, and black often helps to display the style of matching colors. In terms of craftsmanship, compared with straw paintings in other regions, Puyang wheat straw paintings are known for their fine workmanship, burr craft in particular. With this craft as their feature, Puyang straw paintings pursue a delicate, and realistic style. In terms of shape, Puyang wheat straw paintings have absorbed a variety of expression techniques from traditional Chinese painting, paper cutting, embroidery, carving and so on. They use simple lines to express complex things incisively and vividly. The style is simple, and elegant.

3. Appreciation of Wheat Straw Paintings

Nie Yuanzheng is a representative inheritor of the national intangible cultural heritage of wheat straw paintings. His family has been engaged in the production of straw paintings since the Xuande years of the Ming Dynasty and has developed for hundreds of years.

迎春大吉（聂远征）
Good Luck in Spring (Created by Nie Yuanzheng)

第五章　民间美术

"四君子"
"The Four Gentlemen"

The spring jasmine flower and the rooster are combined to form the composition. 鸡（chicken） is homophonic with 吉 (auspicious), so the painting means "Good luck in spring".

"Four gentlemen" are the themes of traditional Chinese culture. They refer to plum blossom, orchid, bamboo and chrysanthemum respectively. The qualities they represent are pride, seclusion, indifference to fame and wealth, and elegance, which have become the symbols for Chinese people to use to express their aspirations.

四、舞阳农民画

1. 舞阳农民画的历史背景

舞阳县隶属河南省漯河市，其境内"贾湖遗址"出土的"骨笛"，反映了早在8000多年前，这里就有了古老的文化艺术。几千年来，生息在舞水岸边的人们，用他们的聪明才智，创造了灿烂辉煌的历史文化。舞阳农民画起源于20世纪50年代，为配合当时的生产运动，全国上下兴起壁画热潮，一些农民一手拿锄头、一手拿画笔，把对美好生活的向往在墙壁上以最简单的漫画形式表现出来。就是在这种以墙壁为载体，以"普罗艺术"为风格的绘画中，通过反复的探索、研究和升华，舞阳农民画于20世纪70年代后期逐步走向成熟。在政府的支持下，先后成立了一批农民画院、农民画经纪公司和农民画专业村，形成了集创作、销售、展示于一体的农民画产业基地，不断提升舞阳农民画的发展规模。

2. 舞阳农民画的艺术特点

舞阳农民画在艺术方向上，一方面继承民间美术传统，它从剪纸、刺绣、民间彩绘和雕塑等民间艺术形式中汲取营养；另一方面融汇现代艺术观念，表现现实生活。舞阳农民画以古朴童稚的人物造型，丰满充实的构图形式，高亢激昂的色彩效果，田园牧歌的鲜活乡情，为画坛所瞩目。

舞阳农民画的题材是现实主义的，它侧重展现人物的情感，表现人与人之间美好和谐的关系，如父母对子女的关爱和生产劳动场面等。但在表现手法上，又善于运用民间美术的夸张、变形和浪漫的想象力。所以舞阳农民画的个性特色还是非常明显，就是浪漫的现实主义。

舞阳农民画家用画笔再现真实的农村生活，但已经不再将视野局限于农村，画家和时代贴合得越来越紧密。《中国日子呱呱叫》《中国梦·和

IV. Wuyang Farmers' Paintings

1. The Historical Background of Wuyang Farmers' Paintings

Wuyang County is under the jurisdiction of Luohe City, Henan Province. The "Bone Flute" unearthed at the "Jiahu Site" in Wuyang County reflects the ancient culture and art that existed here as early as 8000 years ago. For thousands of years, people living on the shore of Wushui have created brilliant history and culture with their intelligence. Wuyang farmers' paintings originated in the 1950s. In line with the production movement at that time, there was a mural craze all over the country. Some farmers held hoes in one hand and paintbrushes in the other hand, and expressed their longing for a better life on the wall in the simplest form of comics. This kind of painting used the wall as the carrier and featured "Pro Art". Through repeated exploration, research and sublimation, Wuyang farmers' paintings gradually matured in the late 1970s. With the support of the government, a number of farmers' painting academies, farmers' painting brokerage companies and villages specializing in farmers' paintings have been established, forming a farmers' painting industry base which integrates creation, sales and display, and constantly improving the development scale of Wuyang farmers' painting.

2. The Artistic Features of Wuyang Farmers' Paintings

In terms of artistic features, on the one hand, Wuyang farmers' paintings inherit the tradition of folk art. They draw nutrition from folk art forms such as paper cutting, embroidery, folk painting and sculpture. On the other hand, they integrate modern art concepts and express real life. Wuyang farmers' paintings have attracted the attention of the painting world with their simple and childish characters, plump and substantial composition, striking and exciting color effects, and the nostalgia of pastoral life.

The theme of Wuyang farmers' paintings is realistic, which focuses on showing the emotions of characters as well as the beautiful and harmonious relationship between people, such as parents' love for their children and the scenes of production and labor. But in terms of expression, Wuyang farmers' paintings

为贵》等一批画作相继而出，画家凭借着对现实生活的敏锐观察，调动夸张的想象，描绘美好生活，承载美好希望，赢得了群众喜爱。

3. 代表性人物及作品

绿荫下（秦春玲）
In the Shade (Created by Qin Chunling)

夏季的夜晚，微风习习，村里的男女老少都跑到树荫底下来乘凉。

这是再平常不过的生活场景。门槛上端坐的守望，她是在给父母、丈夫、孩子还是其他什么人织毛衣？不用问，这些答案都不重要，因为她只是在编制爱。

are good at using the exaggeration, transformation, and romantic imagination of folk art. Therefore, Wuyang farmers' paintings have a very distinctive feature, that is, romantic realism.

Wuyang farmer painters use paintbrushes to reproduce real rural life, but they no longer limit their vision to the countryside. They are keeping pace with the times. A batch of paintings such as *Wonderful Chinese Life*, *Chinese Dream·Harmony Is Precious* have emerged one after another. Wuyang farmer painters have won the love of the masses by virtue of their keen observation of real life, using exaggerated imagination, depicting a better life, and expressing best hopes.

3. Representative Figures and Works

On summer nights, the breeze is blowing. All the men, women and children in the village run to the shade of trees to enjoy the cool.

情系千里（刘志刚）
Affection (Created by Liu Zhigang)

This is an ordinary life scene. Sitting on the threshold, looking around from time to time, is she knitting a sweater for her parents, husband, children, or

夏夜（秦春玲）
Summer Night (Created by Qin Chunling)

土地越来越金贵，粮食只好晒在自家的房顶。夏夜里，一家人干完农活，痛痛快快吃着西瓜，唠着家常，幸福的喜悦爬上了眉梢。

someone else? There is no point asking. None of these answers matters because she is just knitting love.

The land is getting increasingly precious, so the grain has to be dried on the roof of the house. On summer nights, when the family finished their farm work, they happily ate watermelon and chatted about their daily routines. The joy of happiness climbed to their eyebrows.

五、南阳烙花

1. 南阳烙花的历史渊源

南阳烙花具有独特的民族风格和浓郁的地方色彩，它始于清朝光绪年间。据说当时一位名叫赵星三的人在吸大烟时，瘾足兴来，用烧红的烟扦子在烟枪上无意中烙出一幅图画，古色古香，别有情趣。擅画国画的赵星三受到启发，又在冬青木上试烙，居然收到了意想不到的艺术效果。他把这些烙花制品赠送给朋友，朋友们大悦，互相馈赠，一时间成了高雅的礼品。还有人说，烙花艺术是一位清末的小吏所创，这位小吏在闲暇之余，百无聊赖，一天，他灵机一动，用烧红的铁签子在木头上随手烙了几个字赠给同僚，以示风雅。想不到同僚们大为赞赏，前来求字者越来越多，同僚们也群起效仿。极普通的东西，烙上字后，就身价百倍。后来，这种技艺传到民间，人们又加以发展，由单纯的烙字发展到烙画，成为河南南阳一种很有特色的工艺品。

2. 南阳烙花的艺术特点

烙花艺术是用特制的电热笔在木、绸、葫芦等材料上烙绘各种图案，由于烙笔的高温使木板等发糊变色，从而显出线条和轮廓。烙花近似于绘画中的白描，线条流畅，富于变化。画面呈茶褐色，古朴清雅，美观大方。烙花的取材范围也在不断扩大，浩如烟海的传统中国画作品和秀丽的山川风光都成了烙花艺人烙笔下的极好素材。有些烙花艺人再现南阳历史文化名城的风貌，使人们在欣赏烙花这种传统艺术时，对南阳这座古城也有了更深刻的认识。有的艺人用葫芦代替木板、宣纸和绢绸，把平面烙花移到凸凹不平的葫芦上，将烙花艺术和传统观念中的宝葫芦结合起来，这种烙花又有了新的意义。人们在欣赏葫芦烙花的时候，不仅被葫芦上流畅的线条、匀称的色彩所陶醉，同时还为葫芦象征吉祥的

V. Nanyang Pyrography

1. The Historical Origin of Nanyang Pyrography

Nanyang pyrography, with a unique national style and strong local flavor, originated in the reign of Emperor Guangxu in the Qing Dynasty. It is said that at that time, a man named Zhao Xingsan was addicted to smoking a long-stemmed pipe. By accident, he burnt an image on the pipe with a red-hot stick, and it turned out to be antique and interesting. Zhao Xingsan, who was good at traditional Chinese painting, was inspired and tried to burn images into wood, and received unexpected artistic effects. He gave these pyrographic artworks to his friends. They were delighted and gave each other the artworks as gifts. As such, pyrographic artworks became elegant gifts for a time. Some people say that pyrography was created by a petty official in the late Qing Dynasty. In his spare time, the petty official was bored. One day, a good idea occurred to him. He burnt a few words into the wood with a heated poker and gave them to his colleagues to show his elegance. Unexpectedly, his colleagues spoke highly of them and more and more people came to ask for words. His colleagues also followed suit. Very common things, once into which words were burnt, received a tremendous boost in their value. Later, this technique was spread to the ordinary people. They developed it from simple burning words to burning images, which became a very distinctive handicraft in Nanyang, Henan Province.

2. The Artistic Features of Nanyang Pyrography

Pyrography is the art of burning various images onto wood, silk, gourd or other materials with a special electric heating pen. The high temperature leaves burn marks on the wood, thus showing lines and outlines. Pyrography is similar to line drawing in painting, with smooth lines and rich changes. The picture is dark brown, quaint, elegant and appealing. The theme of pyrography artworks is expanding. The vast number of traditional Chinese paintings and beautiful mountains and rivers have become excellent themes for pyrography artists. Some artists reproduce the appearance of the famous historical and cultural City of Nanyang, which enables people to have a deeper understanding of this ancient

含义所喜悦。所以,这种艺术品一出现,就受到了人们的喜爱。

3. 代表作品

解放初期南阳烙花是以烙画筷子为主发展起来的,它选用冬青木,气味清香。在方头筷面上,工匠们用手工烙绘出的画面,典雅精美。

福禄寿
Fu Lu Shou

葫芦谐音"福禄",加之在葫芦表面绘制的寿桃,形成"福禄寿"图案。

牛
Cattle

这是传统木板烙画,风格写实。

city when appreciating the traditional art of pyrography. Some artists use gourds instead of wood, rice paper and silk, burning images on the uneven gourd rather than a flat object. They combine pyrography with the traditional concept of treasure gourds, which lends pyrography a new meaning. When people appreciate the gourd pyrography artworks, they are not only intoxicated by the smooth lines and well-proportioned colors on the gourd, but also delighted by the auspicious meaning of the gourd. Therefore, as soon as this artwork appeared, it was loved by people.

3. Representative Works

烙画筷子
Pyrograph Chopsticks

Nanyang pyrography developed mainly from pyrograph chopsticks in the early days of liberation. They were made of holly wood and had a fragrant smell. On the surface of the square-headed chopsticks, the craftsmen burnt images by hand, which were elegant and exquisite.

Gourd is homophonic with "Fulu" (prosperous posterity, wealth and authority). Together with the longevity peach burnt on the surface of the gourd, the pattern of "Fu Lu Shou" is formed.

This is a traditional wood pyrography artwork with realistic style.

六、开封风筝

1. 开封风筝概况

每到莺飞草长的阳春三月,古都开封又到了郊游踏青、万人竞放风筝的时节。每到这时,上至七十老翁,下到几岁顽童,家家赶制风筝,户户比奇斗彩。此时的古城,哪里空旷,哪里就有放飞者的身影。蓝天碧空之中,点点风筝扶摇直上,五彩缤纷,飘逸逍遥。放风筝者情趣盎然,欢声笑语不断;观风筝者极目远眺,不禁心旷神怡。

"清明节"前后竞放风筝,是开封的古老传统。在北宋画家张择端的《清明上河图》和苏汉臣的《百子游春图》中,都有开封儿童放风筝的情景。旧时的开封,有许多庙会,放风筝也是庙会的一项内容,有时庙会上放风筝的人竟多达千人以上。随着时代的发展,市内庙会虽不存在,但放风筝的习俗却没有因此而湮没,它作为一种古老的传统和开封人的特殊嗜好,一代一代地保留下来。如今的风筝活动分为两种形式:一种是自发的、无意识的民间游戏活动,它和开封人玩斗鸡、戏鸟、养狗一样,成为古城人的古俗;另一种是有组织的风筝比赛,机关和个人都踊跃参加。

2. 开封风筝的分类

开封风筝扎工精细,种类繁多,主要分为六大类:第一类是硬翅风筝。此类风筝以翅膀突出而得名,大的高达数米,小的只有十几厘米。其中的"大脚燕"和"马褂"风筝是硬翅风筝的代表,也是开封风筝独有的品种。"大脚燕"是将燕子加以图案化,把燕子尾巴加以夸张,向两边弯曲,近似两只大脚,因此取名"大脚燕"。这种风筝造型奇特,结构合理,飞行性能良好。第二类风筝是软翅风筝,也就是人们常见的禽鸟风筝,以"鹰""蝴蝶""蜻蜓"等为代表。这类风筝造型逼真、

VI. Kaifeng Kite

1. An Overview of Kaifeng Kite

In the third month of the Chinese lunar calendar each year, when warblers fly and grasses grow, the ancient capital Kaifeng is in the season of outings and flying kites. At this time, from the elderly in their seventies to the naughty kids of a few years old, every family makes kites and competes with each other for the best kite. In the ancient city at this time, where there are open spaces, there are the figures of the kite flyers. In the blue sky, the little kites soar straight up, colorful and flying around at ease. The kite flyers get excited and burst into laughter from time to time. The onlookers gaze into the distance with delight.

Flying kites around the "Qingming Festival" is an ancient tradition in Kaifeng. *In The painting Along the River During the Qingming Festival* by Zhang Zeduan, a painter in the Northern Song Dynasty, and *The painting A Hundred Children Play in Spring* by Su Hanchen, another painter in the Northern Song Dynasty, there are scenes of children in Kaifeng flying kites. In the old Kaifeng, there were many temple fairs, and kite flying was a part of the fair. Sometimes there were more than a thousand people flying kites at the temple fairs. With the development of the times, although temple fairs in the city no longer existed, the custom of flying kites did not disappear. As an ancient tradition and a special hobby of Kaifeng people, it has been passed down from generation to generation. Today's kite flying activities take two forms: One is spontaneous and unconscious folk game activities, which, like Kaifeng people playing cockfighting, playing with birds and raising dogs, has become an ancient custom of people in the ancient city; The other is an organized kite flying competition, in which institutions and individuals participate enthusiastically.

2. The Classification of Kaifeng Kites

Kaifeng kites feature fine craftsmanship and a wide variety. They are classified into six categories. The first category is hard-winged kites. This kind of kite is named for its prominent wings. The large one is as long as several meters, and the small one is only a dozen centimeters long. "Big feet swallow" and "Mandarin

玲珑精致，加以鲜艳的彩绘，外形十分美观。第三类串类风筝的代表是"龙头蜈蚣"，第四类桶形风筝的代表是"宫灯"，第五类板子类风筝的代表是"七星""八卦"等，这些风筝做工复杂，技术要求高，既要有形有色，又要符合力学原理，这就需要有专门技术的能工巧匠们来制作了。近年来，开封又开发出第六类精美的微型风筝，娇小精美，可放于掌上，令人爱不释手，可收藏，还可放飞。开封风筝已成为中外风筝爱好者收藏欣赏的佳品。

3. 代表作品

"宋室风筝"的幌子旗
A Banner Kite of "Songshi Kite"

开封"宋室风筝"造型逼真，画工精美；组装骨架，便于携带；起飞快，不助跑，飞行稳。

老鹰风筝做成活眼、活腿，把鸡毛粘在肚子上，飞上天以后惟妙惟肖，像只真鹰。收线以后滑翔落地，用手接住，就像一只鹰飞落手中。

jacket" kites are the representatives of hard winged kites, and they are also unique to Kaifeng kites. The former adopts the image of a swallow, and the swallow's tail is exaggerated and bent to both sides, similar to two big feet, so it is named "Big feet swallow". This kind of kite has a unique shape, reasonable structure and good flying performance. The second category is the soft-winged kites, which are common bird kites, represented by "eagle" "butterfly" and "dragonfly". This kind of kite is lifelike and exquisite, with bright colors and appealing shape. The third category representative of string kites is the "centipede with a dragon head". The fourth category is the barrel-shaped kites, and the representative of barrel-shaped kites is "Palace lantern", and the fifth category representative of board kites is "Seven stars" "Eight trigrams" and so on. These kites require complex workmanship and excellent skills. They should not only be attractive in shape and color, but also conform to the principle of mechanics. Therefore, only skilled craftsmen with expertise can make them. In recent years, Kaifeng has developed the sixth category miniature kites, which are tiny and exquisite. They can be put on the palm, adorable, collectible and flyable. Kaifeng kites have become a favorite collection for kite lovers at home and abroad.

3. Representative Works

Kaifeng "Songshi Kite" is realistic in shape and exquisite in painting. The framework can be assembled and easy to carry. It does not require run-up, takes off fast and flies steadily.

"宋室风筝" 的老鹰风筝
An Eagle Kite of "Songshi Kite"

"宋室风筝"的"五福闹春"风筝
A "Five Blessings Ushering in the New Year" Kite of "Songshi Kite"

The eyes and legs of the eagle kite are movable, and the chicken feathers are glued to the stomach. After flying into the sky, it is like a real eagle. Once pulled back, the kite glides to a stop. You catch it with your hands, which is just like an eagle flying into your hands.

七、桐柏皮影

1. 皮影艺术的传说

皮影,是民间造型艺术与戏曲艺术巧妙结合而成的综合性艺术品种,在中国各地广泛流传。表演皮影时,艺人在幕布后,一边操纵戏曲人物,一边用当地流行的曲调唱述故事,同时配以打击乐器和弦乐,具有浓厚的乡土气息。河南流传许多关于皮影戏来源的传说。据说,汉武帝最宠爱的李夫人死后,武帝非常思念她,有时竟彻夜难眠。武帝思虑成疾,文武大臣也心急如焚。这时,宫中一个叫李少翁的人,用兽皮雕成李夫人的侧面形象,涂上色彩,模仿李夫人的动作和声音,让汉武帝坐在幕布外面观看。汉武帝惊喜不已,为了满足自己的思念之情,经常让李少翁放映这种影戏。于是,便有了这种以兽皮为主要道具的戏曲形式,这就是今天人们常说的皮影戏。河南现存皮影艺术主要存于豫南桐柏、豫西灵宝和罗山地区。

2. 皮影的制作

皮影的原料多是牛羊皮,豫南喜欢用牛皮,豫西常用驴皮。首先,将皮子炮制、刮薄、磨平,然后,艺人们将各种人物的图谱描绘在上面,用各种型号的刀具刻凿后,再涂抹上颜色。雕刻时,一般都用阳刻,有时也用阴刻,雕工细致,刀法多变。绘图染色也有一定的讲究,女性发饰及衣饰多以花、草、云、凤等纹样为图案,男性则多用龙、虎、水、云等纹样为图案。一般忠良人物为五分面(即正偏影),反面人物为七分面。人物造型和戏曲人物一样,生、旦、净、末、丑角色齐全。制成的皮影高的达 55 厘米,低的仅有 10 厘米左右。皮影人的头和四肢分别雕成,用线连缀而成,以便表演时活动自如。

VII. Tongbai Shadow Puppetry

1. The Legend of Shadow Puppetry

Shadow puppetry is a comprehensive art form that combines folk plastic arts with traditional opera and is widely spread all over China. When performing the shadow play, the puppeteers manipulate the characters in the play (the puppets) behind the curtain while singing the story in local popular tunes, accompanied by percussion instruments and string music instruments. The performance has a strong local flavor. There are many legends about the origin of shadow puppetry in Henan. It is said that after the death of Mrs. Li, the favorite concubine of Emperor Wu of the Han Dynasty, Emperor Wu missed her so much that he sometimes couldn't sleep all night. Eventually he fell ill, and all the ministers were anxious. At this time, a man named Li Shaoweng in the palace carved Mrs. Li's profile out of the animal skin, painted it and imitated Mrs. Li's actions and voice. Emperor Wu was asked to sit outside the curtain to watch. He was pleasantly surprised and in order to ease his missing of Mrs. Li, he often asked Li Shaoweng to perform the shadow play. Thus, this form of opera with animal skins as the main props came into being, which is often called shadow puppetry today. The existing shadow puppetry in Henan mainly scatters in Tongbai in southern Henan, Lingbao in western Henan and Luoshan area.

2. The Making of the Shadow Puppet

Most of the puppets are made of leather from cattle or sheep. Cattle skin is used in Southern Henan, while donkey skin is preferred in Western Henan. First, the leather is processed, scraped and polished. Then, the artists draw various characters on it, carve them out with all kinds of knives, and then paint them. During the carving, usually the carving method Yang is adopted. Sometimes the carving method Yin is used. The carving is meticulous, and the knife technique is changeable. There is also a certain emphasis on painting. Women's hair accessories and clothing are mostly designed with patterns such as flowers, grass, clouds and phoenixes. As for men, patterns like dragons, tigers, water and clouds are widely used. Generally speaking, the loyal and kind characters are carved from a side

3. 皮影赏析

皮影头像
The Profiles of the Shadow Puppets

　　大多采用正侧面的美术造型（即半侧面）。这一技法，俗称"五分相"。我国古代的岩画常用侧面形来画奔跑的猎人与兽。尤其是南阳汉画像石刻，更有很多侧身的形象。皮影艺人最懂得突出剪影，以获得强烈的形象效果。

　　用线条镂空法进行形象刻画，用色简练，平涂着色。在后背光照下，视觉效果剔透而艳丽。

view, with half of their faces being seen (that is, positive partial shadows), while vicious characters are carved with 70% of their faces being seen. The roles in the shadow play are the same as those in the traditional operas. Sheng, Dan, Jing, Mo and Chou are all included. The length of the well-made shadow puppets ranges from 10 centimeters to 55 centimeters. The head and limbs of the shadow puppets are carved separately and connected with lines, so that they can move freely during performances.

3. Appreciation of Shadow Puppets

The head of the shadow puppet mostly adopts the front and side view of the art modeling (i.e., half side). This technique is commonly known as "Wufenxiang"(50% of the face). In ancient Chinese rock paintings, side view was often employed to draw running hunters and beasts, the Stone Carvings of the Han Dynasty in Nanyang in particular, which boasted of many side-looking images. Shadow puppet artists know best how to highlight silhouettes to obtain a strong image effect.

The characters are portrayed by the method of hollowing out the line. Simple color and flat coloring are adopted. In the backlight, the visual effects are clear and gorgeous.

艺人操纵皮影人
A Puppeteer Is Manipulating the Shadow Puppets

人物装束

The Costume of the Characters

生活中的人上肢分为三节：上臂，前臂，手；而桐柏皮影影人的上肢是四节，它把上臂又分为两节。这样的结构有利于增加动作的幅度，增强整个造型的幽默感。

人物装束
The Costume of the Characters

The upper limbs of people in life are divided into three parts: upper arm, forearm and hand. While the upper limbs of the Tongbai shadow puppets are composed of four parts, with the upper arm being further divided into two parts. Such a structure is conducive to increasing the range of action and enhancing the sense of humor of the whole puppet.

八、河南面塑艺术

1. 河南面塑艺术的历史

面塑在我国有着广泛的流传和悠久的历史,最初起源于远古人类的祈福避灾。那时人们要宰杀牲畜为供品,祭奠主宰自然的各路神灵。随着农业的出现和人们对狩猎动物驯养,人们开始使用谷物制成的面粉,做成各种花馍或鱼、羊、牛形,代替牲畜以祭天,这便是面塑的雏形。应该说,在早期,面塑的祭品承载了人与天、地、神、鬼沟通的使命而充满了神秘。当祭祀逐渐延伸到人类对自然神的感激、对先祖的拜祭和对人生重要时刻的仪式,面塑供品就到了既表达虔诚又可食用的民俗时期。到了明朝中叶,面塑便出现了祭典与欣赏的功能分化。作为供品的面塑,适用广泛而较为粗制;而具欣赏功能的面塑逐渐衍变成一种技艺而独立。它用特殊的面料(可以长时间放置、不食)捏塑成五彩缤纷的儿童玩具和室内摆设品,供人们把玩和欣赏。

2. 河南面塑艺术的主要类型

（1）面花

面花其实就是花馍艺术,它和民间节日、民间礼仪结合得十分紧密。从民间节日方面来说,民间盛行"二十八,蒸花花",指的就是腊月二十八蒸花馍的活动。每到这天,巧妇们各展绝技,普通的面团经过拉、捏、揉、叠,顷刻之间,妇女们就把它塑成了"二龙戏珠""丹凤朝阳""鲤鱼跳龙门"等花馍,蒸熟后再涂上色彩,花花绿绿十分好看,让节日的气氛更加浓烈。面花在礼尚往来中的作用,比其在节日中还要重要。在婚丧嫁娶、生老病死等重大活动中,几乎都离不开面塑艺术品。如阴历六月,豫北有舅舅给外甥送面羊的风俗;老人寿诞之时,晚辈要给老人篆一个桃形寿馍,祝福老人健康长寿。总体而言,豫西和豫东的

VIII. Henan Dough Sculpture Art

1. The History of Henan Dough Sculpture Art

Dough sculpture is widely spread in China and enjoys a long history. It originated from ancient people's praying for blessings and warding off disasters. At that time, people slaughtered livestock to serve as sacrifices to the gods who ruled the nature. With the emergence of agriculture and the domestication of hunting animals, people began to use flour made from grains to make various steamed buns or fish, sheep and cattle to replace livestock to worship Heaven. This is the prototype of dough sculpture. It should be said that in the early days, the offerings of dough sculptures carried the mission of communicating with heaven, earth, gods and ghosts and were full of mystery. When the sacrifice gradually extended to human beings' gratitude to the gods of nature, worship to ancestors and rituals for important moments in life, dough sculpture offerings entered a folk custom period during which they were not only used to express devoutness but also edible. In the middle of the Ming Dynasty, there appeared a functional differentiation between sacrifice and appreciation. The dough sculptures which served as offerings were widely used and relatively crude, while the dough sculptures with the function of appreciation had gradually evolved into a kind of art and became independent. The latter were made of special dough (durable and inedible) and kneaded into colorful children's toys and indoor decorations for people to play with and appreciate.

2. The Main Types of Henan Dough Sculpture Art

(1) Mianhua

Mianhua is actually the art of *huamo* (a kind of decorated steamed bun, usually in the shape of various flowers and animals), which is closely connected with folk festivals and folk rituals. From the perspective of folk festivals, the popular "二十八，蒸花花" refers to "The activity of steaming buns on the twenty-eighth day of the twelfth lunar month". On this day, the clever women show their unique skills. After pulling, kneading, pinching

面花
A Mianhua

花馍精巧细腻、色彩鲜艳，豫北、豫南和豫中的花馍朴素大方、浑厚丰满。

（2）面人

李金城是中原地区面塑艺术传承人，中央级多家媒体报道过"面人李"的作品及事迹。他有过多次转行的机会，可心里始终丢不下面塑，可以说，他的一生是把生命揉进了面里，塑出了他执着和真诚的壮丽画卷。他的面塑造型矫健优美，人物强调个性，以文物官员、忠臣良将、民俗事象、戏曲人物为主，做工尤为精到，色彩丰富但艳而不俗，作品长期保存不霉不变形。

and folding, the women instantly shape the ordinary dough into *huamo* such as "Two dragons playing with the pearl" "Phoenix facing the sun" and "A carp jumping over the Dragon Gate". After being steamed, they are painted with various colors, making the festive atmosphere more intense. Mianhua plays a more important role in the exchange of gifts than in festivals. Major activities such as weddings and funerals, birth and death, all call for dough sculptures. For example, in the sixth lunar month, there is a custom in the Northern Henan that an uncle sends a dough sculpture sheep to his nephew; On the birthday of an old person, the younger generation should give the old person a peach-shaped birthday bun, wishing him a long and healthy life. In general, *huamo* in the Western and Eastern Henan is exquisite and colorful, while *huamo* in Northern, Southern Henan and Central Henan is simple and round.

(2) Mianren

Li Jincheng is the inheritor of dough sculpture art in the Central Plains. Many central media have reported the artworks and deeds of "Mianren Li".

面塑

Dough Sculpture

面塑王昭君（中国古代四大美女之一）
The Dough Sculpture Wang Zhaojun (One of the Four Beauties in Ancient China)

Chapter 5 Folk Art

老寿星

The God of Longevity

He had many opportunities to change his profession, but he could not give up his obsession with dough sculptures. It can be said that he has kneaded his whole life into the dough lumps, making magnificent dough sculptures with his persistence and sincerity. His dough sculptures are vigorous and graceful, and the characters have distinct personalities. They are cultural relics officials, loyal ministers, outstanding generals, and the characters appearing in the folk customs and traditional operas. The workmanship is particularly exquisite. The colors are rich but not vulgar, and the artworks can be preserved for a long time without mold and deformation.

九、苏家作龙凤灯

1. 苏家作龙凤灯的基本情况

苏家作村位于河南博爱县,博爱县盛产竹子,编制业繁盛,有竹编、草编、荆编、柳编和苇编,其中竹编最为发达。早在明末清初的时候,竹编就远销海内外。随着经济的发展,竹编手艺遍布县城的所有村庄。竹编手艺促进了龙凤灯的制作,成为花灯制作的基础。

制作花灯是当地的习俗,每当元宵节时,各家各户都会制作龙灯、老虎灯、麒麟灯、孔雀灯、鱼灯、荷花灯等悬挂在自家门口。每年春节和火神庙庙会期间,苏家作的村民都会依据传统民间故事制作各式各样的花灯,祛病除灾,以庆祝丰收之年,祈求来年能有一个好收成。到了清道光年间,博爱县举办大耍灯比赛,苏家作人毋黑旦为了能拔头筹,别出心裁,依据"龙凤呈祥"的民间传统故事制作出凤灯,并与龙灯结合,龙凤灯形成。龙灯和凤灯结合的首次表演,获得了好评,取得了佳

龙灯和凤灯

The Dragon Lantern and the Phoenix Lantern

IX. Sujiazuo Dragon and Phoenix Lanterns

1. The Basic Information About Sujiazuo Dragon and Phoenix Lanterns

Sujiazuo Village is in Boai County, Henan Province. Boai County is rich in bamboo and the weaving industry is booming. There are bamboo weaving, straw weaving, Vitex weaving, willow weaving and reed weaving, of which bamboo weaving is the most developed. As early as the late Ming and early Qing Dynasties, bamboo weaving products were sold at home and abroad. With the development of the economy, bamboo weaving craft has spread all over the villages in the county, which has promoted the production of dragon and phoenix lanterns and become the basis for the production of lanterns.

Making lanterns is a local custom. During the Lantern Festival, every household will make various lanterns such as dragon lanterns, tiger lanterns, kylin lanterns, peacock lanterns, fish lanterns and lotus lanterns to hang at their doorsteps. During the Spring Festival and the Fire Temple Fair every year, the villagers of Sujiazuo make all kinds of lanterns based on traditional folk tales to ward off diseases and disasters and pray for a good harvest in the coming year. In the Daoguang period of the Qing Dynasty, Boai County held a lantern performance competition. To win the first prize, Wu Heidan, a villager of Sujiazuo, created a phoenix lantern based on the folk tale of "dragon and phoenix bring prosperity", and combined it with the dragon lantern to form a dragon and phoenix Lantern. The first performance of the combination of the Dragon lantern and the phoenix lantern was well received and successful, which has been followed ever since. Later, Wu Heidan added more than a dozen kinds of lanterns, such as spider lantern, sun lantern, white cloud lantern, bird lantern and Tangyuan lantern, arranged many lantern dance performances which were based on folk tales. During the Sujiazuo Fire Temple Fair every year, more than 200 people perform the dragon and phoenix lantern dance together, and the scene is extremely spectacular.

绩，从此便沿袭下来。后来，毋黑旦在此基础上，增加了蜘蛛灯、太阳灯、白云灯、百鸟灯、汤圆灯等十几种灯，根据民间故事编排了很多灯舞节目。每年苏家作火神庙庙会期间，200多人一起表演龙凤灯舞，场面极为壮观。

2. 苏家作龙凤灯的制作

苏家作民间艺人创造出各种各样的龙凤灯造型，其造型夸张，形象生动。经过100多年的变迁，龙凤灯的造型不仅只是"子承父业"，更多的是民间艺人心灵的创造。现在龙凤灯造型是在原有造型的基础上进行了改良，融入了很多现代化的新材料，在增加了视觉美感的同时，延长了龙凤灯的使用寿命。龙灯的制作主要有以下几个步骤：首先选取竹子扎龙的骨架，外面糊好彩色布条作龙皮，艺人们用颜料作龙皮上画上龙鳞，起到画龙点睛的效果。龙脊缝制多个三角相连的形状，每个三角形里都塞上满满的棉花，让龙脊更立体。龙腹系有45个铃铛，跑起来叮当作响。最复杂的是龙头的制作，有几十道工序。制作龙头的材料很多是旧物再利用，如龙牙用白色泡沫制作而成，再涂上颜色；龙眼大多用旧灯泡或者塑料瓶，外面画上黑色的眼珠和红色的眼眶，使其更加逼真。龙脊上装有烟花燃放装置，内部还装有LED灯，晚上表演时整条龙都是亮堂堂的。

龙灯可燃放焰火
The Dragon Lanterns Can Set Off Fireworks.

2. The Making of Sujiazuo Dragon and Phoenix Lantern

The folk craftsmen in Sujiazuo have created a variety of Dragon and Phoenix shapes, which are exaggerated and vivid. After more than 100 years of changes, the shape of the succeeding dragon and phoenix lantern is more a new creation of the folk craftsmen than a copy of the preceding one. Now the shape of the dragon and phoenix lantern is improved on the basis of the original one, and many modern new materials are integrated, which not only increases the lantern's visual beauty, but also extends its service life. The making of a dragon lantern mainly includes the following steps: First, select proper bamboo to make the skeleton of the dragon, and paste colored cloth strips on the outside to serve as the dragon skin. Then the craftsmen use paint to draw the dragon scales on the skin, which makes the dragon more vivid. The dragon's spine is sewn with a number of triangles connected to each other, and each triangle is stuffed with cotton to make the dragon's spine more lifelike. There are 45 bells tied to the belly of the dragon, which jingle when the dragon runs. The most complicated part is the making of the dragon head, which entails dozens of procedures. Many of the materials used to make the dragon head are old things. For instance, the dragon's teeth are made of white foam and then painted; the dragon's eyes are mostly made of old light bulbs or plastic bottles, with black eyeballs and red eye sockets painted on the outside to make them more realistic. The dragon's ridge is equipped with a fireworks display device and LED lights inside so that the whole dragon is brightly lit during the performance at night.

3. 苏家作龙凤灯的艺术特色

苏家作人充分调动想象力，创造出巧夺天工的龙凤灯造型。苏家作龙凤灯的审美特征体现在三个方面：其一是"大""乐"之美。龙凤灯舞追求大道具、大场面、大动作，这种"大"使人们感受到崇高的美，引起人们惊叹，从而获得审美的愉悦。其二是吉祥之美。龙凤灯的造型、色彩和内容，都讲究吉祥，"龙凤呈祥"寄托着人们美好的愿望，体现了一种积极向上的生活态度。其三是生命之美。龙凤灯舞大量象征"阴阳"的内容表现了"生生"观念，揭示出人们对生命的热爱。

3. The Artistic Features of Sujiazuo Dragon and Phoenix Lanterns

The craftsmen in Sujiazuo give their imagination a full play and create a wonderful dragon and phoenix lantern shape. The aesthetic characteristics of Sujiazuo dragon and phoenix lanterns are reflected in three aspects. The first one is the beauty of "big" and "happy". The dragon and phoenix lantern dance pursues big props, big scenes, and big movements. This kind of "big" makes people feel the sublime beauty and lets them marvel, obtaining aesthetic pleasure. The second one is the beauty of auspiciousness. The shape, color and content of the dragon and phoenix lanterns are all auspicious. The saying "Dragon and phoenix bring prosperity" expresses people's good wishes and embodies a cheerful outlook towards life. The third one is the beauty of life. The dragon and phoenix lantern dance has a lot of content symbolizing "Yin and Yang", which expresses the concept of "Life and Growth" and reveals people's love for life.

十、修武绞胎瓷

1. 修武绞胎瓷的历史发展

绞胎釉瓷,产于修武,源于唐代,是唐代陶瓷业中的一个新工艺。北宋时,绞胎瓷在修武当阳峪实现了大规模生产,绞胎工艺更趋成熟,有席编纹、麦穗纹、羽毛纹、回转纹、木旋纹、流沙纹等10多种纹理的变化。北宋末靖康之变后绞胎瓷消亡数百年。1981年,北京故宫博物院珍藏的两件当阳峪宋代绞胎瓷引起了中央工艺美院梅健鹰教授的极大兴趣,他亲临实地考证、试制,对失传的绞胎瓷工艺中几种不同的绞胎纹理进行开发,使其得以复苏。2001年,河南省科技部门将当阳绞胎瓷工艺当作科技攻关项目,对其进行全面开发,成功烧制出当代优质的绞胎艺术瓷。

2. 修武绞胎瓷的制作工艺

所谓绞胎,是将两种或两种以上不同颜色的瓷土糅合在一起,然后相绞拉坯,制作成形。然后浇一层透明釉,进行烧制,入窑后产生行云流水般的奇异纹饰效果,又称透花瓷。由于泥坯绞揉的方式不同,纹理变化亦无穷,常见的有木纹、鸟羽纹、云纹、流水纹等,有的如老树缠绕盘根错节,有的如层山叠嶂起伏不定,构思奇巧,变化万千。绞胎陶瓷每一件产品都有其不同的纹理特色,其纹理结构只有相似,没有相同。它以独特的纹理结构和色彩变化在陶瓷领域独树一帜,堪称制瓷精品。

X. Xiuwu Jiaotai Porcelain

1. The Historical Development of Xiuwu Jiaotai Porcelain

Jiaotai porcelain, produced in Xiuwu and originated in the Tang Dynasty, is a new craft in the ceramics industry in the Tang Dynasty. In the Northern Song Dynasty, the mass production of Jiaotai porcelain was achieved in Dangyangyu, Xiuwu. The craft of Jiaotai became more mature, with more than 10 kinds of texture changes, such as mat weaving pattern, ear of wheat pattern, feather pattern, rotary pattern, wood swirl pattern, quicksand pattern, and so on. After the Jingkang revolution at the end of the Northern Song Dynasty, Jiaotai porcelain disappeared for hundreds of years. In 1981, two pieces of Dangyangyu Song Dynasty Jiaotai porcelain collected by the Palace Museum in Beijing aroused Mei Jianying's great interest, who was the professor of the Central Academy of Arts and Crafts. He personally went to the field for research and trial production, and developed several different textures which used to exist in the lost Jiaotai porcelain craft, so that Jiaotai porcelain was revived. In 2001, the Science and Technology Department of Henan Province took Dangyang Jiaotai porcelain craft as a key scientific and technological project, comprehensively developed it, and successfully fired contemporary high-quality Jiaotai art porcelain.

2. The Production Process of Xiuwu Jiaotai Porcelain

The so-called Jiaotai is to mix two or more assorted colors of porcelain clay together, and then twist and pull the embryo to make it into shape. Then pour a layer of transparent glaze and fire it. After entering the kiln, it produces a strange decorative effect like clouds and flowing water. So Jiaotai porcelain is also called transparent flower porcelain. Due to the different ways of twisting and kneading the clay, the textures change infinitely. The common ones are wood grain, bird feather pattern, cloud pattern, flowing water pattern, etc. Some are like old trees with intertwined roots, and some are like rolling mountains with ups and downs, ingenious and diverse. Each product of Jiaotai ceramics has its own different texture characteristics, and its texture structure is only similar to each other, but not the same. It is unique in the field of ceramics with its distinctive texture

3. 作品欣赏

丝绸之路（柴战柱）
The Silk Road (Created by Chai Zhanzhu)

structure and color changes, can be called a fine porcelain.

3. Appreciation of the Artworks

蒜头瓶
A Garlic Bottle

十一、安阳苏奇灯笼

1. 安阳苏奇灯笼的基本情况

苏奇灯笼因产于安阳县永和乡苏奇村而得名。在甲骨文出土故地安阳县,有一种不知流传了多少年的元宵习俗,从正月十三直到十七,一到晚上,家家父母陪孩子到街上玩灯笼。在五彩缤纷的灯笼中,"苏奇灯笼"最有名,以其造型古朴、灯笼画内容寓意深刻,价格便宜,深受百姓喜爱。除了元宵佳节,这种灯笼也用于日常的生产和生活之中,当地农民过去起早贪黑拾粪时打灯笼,所以苏奇灯笼又有个俗称叫"拾粪灯"。

苏奇灯笼俗称"拾粪灯"
Suqi Lanterns Are Commonly Known as "Dung Collecting Lanterns".

2. 安阳苏奇灯笼的制作技艺

苏奇灯笼制作的第一步是画彩画,先用刻有戏曲人物的雕版在裁好的白纸上拓印出黑线轮廓,然后将原色红、黄、紫、蓝加水调配成水颜料,手工填色。整个画面色彩对比鲜明,朴实无华,厚重清朗。第二步用高粱穗茎扎制成六七寸高、四寸宽的骨架,把事先印好的彩画裱糊在上面,然后放在通风的地方晾干。最后,为了美观起见,还要在灯笼的

XI. Anyang Suqi Lanterns

1. An Overview of Anyang Suqi Lanterns

Suqi lanterns are named after Suqi Village, Yonghe Town, Anyang County, where they are produced. In Anyang County, where the oracle bone inscriptions were unearthed, there is a custom about the Lantern Festival that has been passed down for many years. From the 13th day to the 17th day of the first lunar month, parents in almost every family accompany their children to take to the streets to play with lanterns at night. Among the colorful lanterns, "Suqi lanterns" are the most famous. They are deeply loved by the local people because of their simple shape, the profound meaning of the paintings on the outside of the lanterns and low price. In addition to the Lantern Festival, this kind of lantern is also used in daily production and life. Local farmers used to take lanterns when picking up dung in the early morning and evening, so Suqi lanterns are also commonly known as "Dung collecting lanterns".

2. The Making of Anyang Suqi Lanterns

The first step in making Suqi lanterns is to paint pictures. First, use the board engraved with opera characters to print the black outline on the well-cut white paper, and then add water to mix the primary colors of red, yellow, purple and blue into water pigments, and paint the characters manually. The whole painting is plain, thick and clear, with the colors forming a sharp contrast. The second step is to tie sorghum stalks into a skeleton six or seven inches high and four inches wide, paste the color pictures on it, and then put it in a ventilated place to dry. Finally, for the sake of beauty, draw lines on each frame of the lantern to make it look unsophisticated.

各个边框画上线条，使之看起来整体大方，古拙淳朴。

灯笼画
Paintings on the Lanterns

3. 安阳苏奇灯笼的艺术价值

　　苏奇灯笼的艺术价值在于那一幅幅手工描绘的灯笼图画，画面表现内容丰富，人物特征鲜明，形式风格独特，极具观赏价值、文化价值和学术价值。灯笼画多以京剧、豫剧中的戏曲人物和民间传说人物为主，内容有《古城会》《桃园三结义》《三打白骨精》等。后来为适应时代要求，又在灯笼画中增加了新的戏曲题材，如《沙家浜》《红灯记》《智取威虎山》等。苏奇灯笼画的画面内容以独特的艺术形式对调理民风、教化群众发挥着一定作用。除了戏曲人物造型外，灯笼画中还有许多群众喜闻乐见的花卉、飞禽走兽等，借以表达吉祥、喜庆的含意和美好的祝愿。

3. The Artistic Value of Anyang Suqi Lanterns

The artistic value of Suqi lanterns lies in the hand-painted pictures, which are rich in content, distinctive in characters, unique in form and style, and have great ornamental, cultural and academic value. Most of the pictures on the lanterns are based on the characters in folklore or characters in Peking Opera and Henan Opera, such as *Sworn Brothers*, *Brotherhood Forged in the Peach Garden*, *Monkey King Subdues the White-Bone Spirit Thrice*. Later, in order to meet the requirements of the times, new opera themes were added to the lantern paintings, for instance, *Shajiabang*, *The Legend of the Red Lantern* and *Taking Tiger Mountain by Strategy* and so on. The content of Suqi lantern paintings play a certain role in regulating folk customs and civilizing the masses in a unique artistic form. In addition to the characters in the traditional Chinese operas, there are many flowers, birds and animals loved by the masses in the lantern paintings to express auspicious and festive meanings and good wishes.

结　语

《中原民俗》属于"中华源·河南故事"中外文系列丛书中的一种。本属于重要民俗的陶瓷、豫菜、武术、神话等内容，丛书内都有专书，相互参看，读者自然能获得关于中原民俗的完整印象。

《中原民俗》共分为五个部分。前三个部分讲天地人的生命节奏。天地节奏是人感知到的，人生节奏是人经历过的。时间是有节奏的，节庆是时间节奏的展演。空间是有节奏的，庙会是空间节奏的展演。人生是有节奏的，出生、婚姻、丧葬等礼仪是人生节奏的展演。在每一个关节点，都要沟通神灵，确定发展方向。后两个部分讲人运用自身的创造力，将天地人的生命节奏表现在人所创造的建筑、雕塑、绘画等作品中。建筑是凝固的音乐，是生命节奏的外显。每一件美术作品都是质料性质的提纯，是人心的外化。民俗带着土气，是从土地里生长出来的文明之花。中原人的生活节奏和生活空间是与土地联系在一起的，每一代人站在中原土地上，看到土肥水美，植被丰茂，禽兽杂多，都愿意脚下生根，把自己扎入这片土地；感受到北温带春夏秋冬四季变化的清晰节奏，都乐意将自己的生命弹奏成为这个节奏的和弦。日出月落，春种秋收，中原人土里刨食，优良的自然条件帮助人们获得稳定的收成，人与土地的牢固关系养成了厚道忠诚的人品；按时节展开的劳动，将人的生命节奏融入自然的节奏里。技艺民俗花样百出，一把泥土，就能够玩出许多花样，可以制作成日用陶瓷、建筑砖瓦，甚至有声有色的小儿玩具。衣食住行，生老病死，婚丧嫁娶，生活民俗的内容紧贴生命生活，形式简单而元气充盈，充满热情与欢乐。"壤非壤不高，水非水不流"（《逸周书·文儆》），中原大地起高峰，每一粒土旮旯都不是多余的。垒土成山，才能登高望远。中原民俗需要有架构，有安排，有传承，有系统，还有许多提升品质、扩展规模、加强影响的工作要做。

Concluding Remarks

Folklore of the Central Plains is one of the series of "The Source of China · Henan Stories". Ceramics, Henan cuisine, martial arts, myths and other contents are important parts of folk customs. There are special books on them in this series. By referring to each other, readers will naturally get a complete impression of the folk customs in the Central Plains.

Folklore of the Central Plains is divided into five parts. The first three parts focus on the life rhythm of Heaven, earth and man. The rhythm of Heaven and earth is perceived by people, and the rhythm of life is experienced by people. Time has a rhythm, and festivals are the performances of the rhythm of time. Space has a rhythm, and temple fairs are the performances of the rhythm of space. Life has a rhythm, and rituals such as birth, marriage, and funeral are the performances of the rhythm of life. At every crucial point, human beings should communicate with gods and determine the direction of development. The last two parts evolve around people's using their own creativity to express the life rhythm of heaven, earth and man through the works of architecture, sculpture, painting and so on. Architecture is frozen music and the manifestation of the rhythm of life. Every artwork is the purification of the nature of the materials used and the externalization of the human heart. Folk customs are rustic and they are the flowers of civilization that grow from the land. The pace of life and living space of the people in the Central plains are linked to the land. Every generation who stands on the land of the Central Plains and sees the fertile soil, beautiful water, lush vegetation and miscellaneous animals is willing to settle down in this land. Feeling the clear rhythm of the seasonal changes in the northern temperate zone, they are willing to become the chords that go with the rhythm. With the passage of time and the change of four seasons, people in the Central Plains get food from the soil. The excellent natural conditions help people obtain a stable harvest. The firm relationship between people and the land has cultivated a kind and loyal character. Labor in line with the solar terms integrates the rhythm of human life into the rhythm of nature. Folk arts take numerous forms. A handful of mud can be transformed into many things, such as daily-use ceramics, building

这是一本多人合作完成的书。有领导的整体规划，有责任编辑的督促审查，有中文作者和外语译者的分工协作，有美术作者的用心配图。中文作者三人，霍志刚负责中原庙会、人生礼仪和建筑民俗部分，张敏负责民间美术部分，罗家湘负责前言、结语和节庆民俗部分，并最终统稿。我们的作品只是中原民俗高山上的一粒土，要认识中原民俗之美，还请你自己亲自来中原走走看看。

bricks, and even vivid children's toys. Folk customs cover a wide range of aspects, from clothing, food, housing and transportation, life and death to weddings and funerals, which are all closely related to life. The forms of folk customs are simple and full of vitality, and joy. "Soil is not high without soil, and water is not flowing without water" (*Yi Zhou Shu·Wen Jing*). The land in the Central Plains rises to a peak, and every grain of soil is not redundant. Only when the soil is built into a mountain can you climb high and look far. The folk customs in the Central Plains need a structure, arrangement, inheritance and system, and there is still much work to be done to improve the quality, expand the scale and strengthen the influence.

This is a collaborative book. It involves the overall planning of the leaders, the supervision and review of responsible editors, the division of labor and cooperation between the Chinese authors and the foreign language translators, and the hard work of the illustrators. There are three Chinese authors. Huo Zhigang is responsible for the parts concerning Temple Fairs in the Central Plains, Rites, and Architectural Folklore. Zhang Min is responsible for the parts concerning Folk Art. Luo Jiaxiang is responsible for the Preface, Concluding Remarks and parts relating to Festival Folklore, and the final draft. Our book is just a grain of soil on the mountain of folk customs in the Central Plains. To fully understand the beauty of folk customs in the Central Plains, please come here and have a look for your own.

附录：中国历史年代简表
Appendix: A Brief Chronology of Chinese History

中国历史年代简表
A Brief Chronology of Chinese History

五帝时代 Period of the Five Legendary Rulers c. 2600 BC-c. 2070 BC	黄帝 Huangdi (Yellow Emperor)	
	颛顼 Zhuanxu	
	帝喾 Diku (Emperor Ku)	
	尧 Yao	
	舜 Shun	
夏 Xia Dynasty	c. 2070 BC-c. 1600 BC	
商 Shang Dynasty	c. 1600 BC-c. 1046 BC	
西周 Western Zhou Dynasty	c. 1046 BC-c. 771 BC	
东周 Eastern Zhou Dynasty 770 BC-256 BC	春秋 Spring and Autumn Period	770 BC-476 BC
	战国 Warring States Period	475 BC-221 BC
秦 Qin Dynasty	221 BC-206 BC	
汉 Han Dynasty 206 BC-220 AD	西汉 Western Han	206 BC-25 AD
	东汉 Eastern Han	25 AD-220 AD
三国 Three Kingdoms 220 AD-280 AD	魏 Wei	220 AD-265 AD
	蜀汉 Shu Han	221 AD-263 AD
	吴 Wu	222 AD-280 AD
晋 Jin Dynasty 265 AD-420 AD	西晋 Western Jin	265 AD-317 AD
	东晋 Eastern Jin	317 AD-420 AD

续表 Continued Table

南北朝 Southern and Northern Dynasties 420 AD-589 AD	南朝 Southern Dynasties	宋 Song	420 AD-479 AD
		齐 Qi	479 AD-502 AD
		梁 Liang	502 AD-557 AD
		陈 Chen	557 AD-589 AD
	北朝 Northern Dynasties	北魏 Northern Wei	386 AD-534 AD
		东魏 Eastern Wei	534 AD-550 AD
		北齐 Northern Qi	550 AD-577 AD
		西魏 Western Wei	535 AD-556 AD
		北周 Northern Zhou	557 AD-581 AD
隋 Sui Dynasty		581 AD-618 AD	
唐 Tang Dynasty		618 AD-907 AD	
五代十国 Five Dynasties and Ten States	五代 Five Dynasties 907 AD-960 AD	后梁 Later Liang	907 AD-923 AD
		后唐 Later Tang	923 AD-936 AD
		后晋 Later Jin	936 AD-947 AD
		后汉 Later Han	947 AD-950 AD
		后周 Later Zhou	951 AD-960 AD
	十国 Ten States 902 AD-979 AD	北汉 Northern Han	951 AD-979 AD
		吴 Wu	902 AD-937 AD
		吴越 Wuyue	907 AD-978 AD
		闽 Min	909 AD-945 AD
		南汉 Southern Han	917 AD-971 AD
		荆南（又称"南平"）Jingnan (Nanping)	924 AD-963 AD
		楚 Chu	927 AD-951 AD
		南唐 Southern Tang	937 AD-975 AD
		前蜀 Former Shu	907 AD-925 AD
		后蜀 Later Shu	934 AD-965 AD

续表 Continued Table

宋 Song Dynasty 960 AD-1279 AD	北宋 Northern Song	960 AD-1127 AD
	南宋 Southern Song	1127 AD-1279 AD
辽 Liao (契丹 Qidan/Khitan)	907 AD-1125 AD	
西夏 Xixia (Tangut)	1038 AD-1227 AD	
金 Jin	1115 AD-1234 AD	
元 Yuan Dynasty	1206 AD-1368 AD	
明 Ming Dynasty	1368 AD-1644 AD	
清 Qing Dynasty	1616 AD-1911 AD	
中华民国 Republic of China	1912 AD-1949 AD	
中华人民共和国 People's Republic of China	1949 AD-